Jon

Wishing you many years
of great fishing.

Tom

Bonefish B. S.

and Other Good Fish Stories

Tom Davidson

Contributing Authors:
Stu Apte, Don Bowers, Bill Curtis, Chico Fernandez,
Dr. Robert Humston, Sandy Moret, Billy Pate and Steve Venini

HUDSON BOOKS

Book design by:
The Floating Gallery
www.thefloatinggallery.com

Printed in Canada

Tom Davidson
Bonefish B. S. and Other Good Fish Stories

1. Author   2. Title   3. Fishing

ISBN: 0-9762502-7-6
LCCN: 2004116173

TABLE OF CONTENTS

PREFACE

Let's settle one matter right up front. This book is being motivated out of love for the sport and not out of any distorted perception or delusions related to my fishing skills or knowledge. The proceeds from the book will go to support the research programs and other activities of Bonefish & Tarpon Unlimited (BTU).

BTU is an organization committed to the nurturing and enhancement of bonefish and tarpon fisheries worldwide through research, education and regulation. The Founding members of this group (listed in the appendix) read like a Who's Who of shallow saltwater fishing. I believe BTU will play a major role in directing and funding research, regulations, and fish management that will be key to the survival of this fantastic sport.

Saltwater sport fishing is not only a very challenging and enjoyable pastime, but it also represents significant commercial activity estimated at over $750 million per year in the State of Florida alone in year 2000 dollars. Ironically in spite of the commercial implications of the sport and the number of people pursuing their passion, very little is actually known about the behavior of bonefish (Albula vulpes) or the other seven species of bonefish, their life cycle, habitat, and most important, factors that limit the adult population.

This dedicated group of BTU supporters are committed to change this with an end objective to be sure this enjoyable sport will be enjoyed by our grandchildren and their grandchildren.

I am deeply indebted and most appreciative of the many BTU Founders who helped me with information for this book, especially George Hommell and Stu Apte. Also, I am most appreciative of the contributed chapters by legendary anglers Stu Apte, Chico Fernandez, Sandy Moret, and Billy Pate, and legendary guides Bill Curtis and Don Bowers. A special thank you to my assistant Susan Graham for her long hours of deciphering my handwriting and bad photography, to my daughter-in-law Michelle Davidson for her expert proofreading and editing assistance, and to my personal captain / guide Steve Venini for his work in putting together the fly tying information and photos.

I also wish to acknowledge the information from the many fine bonefish publication as noted in the bibliography and to Frontiers for their assistance in digging out many of the photos on where to fish destinations.

I dedicate this book to my wife who patiently suffers through my bonefishing and to my sons who can no doubt fish rings around their father.

CHAPTER I

Early Days and the Evolution
of Fly Fishing for Bonefish

Exactly when the first bonefish was caught or where, no one seems to know for sure and there are no official records to check. No doubt it was well before 1900 and probably not by intention. It may well have been someone fishing for sea trout in the bay who hooked onto a more lively fight than expected or even someone bottom fishing on the reefs in the Florida Keys on a cool winter day when the bonefish had moved from the flats to the warmer waters near the gulf stream to stay warm. Or maybe it was caught by a local Bahamian who was angling a line for a nice snapper dinner.

One thing is for sure, whoever and whenever it was; they hooked onto a fight beyond their expectation. Then too, there was probably a point in time when bonefish were pursued with hook or net as food. In fact, even early Florida Keys guides kept and cooked or sold their catch into the early 60's. However, in recent times bonefish are much more revered, and they are now pursued as a challenging hook-up because they render a very sporty and rewarding fight when successfully hooked.

Regrettably there are still many places where bonefish are still pursued as food, or even worse, as bait. I have personally seen them for sale in the fish markets of Mahe, Seychelles, and watched them being netted by the dozen in tidal creeks at low tide in Christmas Island. There have even been prominent saltwater magazines with articles about using bonefish as marlin bait as recently as the late 1990's. For any fisherman who has spent a half day or more without finding a fish, this is a real heartbreak scenario.

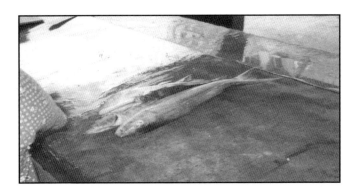

Local fish market in the Seychelles.

Getting back to the beginning, in the 1890's sport fishing was both active and organized in the lower Florida Keys. Northern yachtsmen would motor or sail down to the Keys to pursue warm weather, excellent bill fishing in the gulf stream, and in-shore and back country fishing on their dinghy's. They chose the Keys because there they could find a change of pace and they could avoid weather that made offshore fishing uncomfortable.

Long Key Club was one institution that was not only a gathering spot for sport fishermen, but assumed the role of record keeper of those early catches deserving of notation. Regrettably the Long Key Club and all of its records were blown away in the hurricane of 1935. Among the many rich and famous attracted to this emerging sport was the famous author and lecturer, Zane Grey.

Once fishing for bonefish as a target species did start, it attracted an addicted group of followers. In the early days, the bait of choice was a finny crab or hermit crab which the fish liked just fine. Crabs took preference over shrimp, not because the fish liked them better, but because shrimp were hard to come by in those days, as recreational fishing in the Keys was not well enough developed to support a full network of bait catchers and sellers.

The earliest reliable records I have been able to locate suggest that a basic form of guide-supported fishing was available in the Florida Keys at the Matecumbe Hotel in the 1920's. The Matecumbe Hotel owned by Mrs. Ed Bitters would arrange guides. There was also a free-lance guide operation run by Dr. Lenard Woods in that same area.

The Lodge, Long Key Fishing Club c. 1925

Long Key, Florida MM 66 c. 1920

The cottages at Long Key Club
(Photos courtesy of Florida Keys Historical Society)

The Matecumbe Hotel was at Mile Marker 81.5 today

Remains of the Matecumbe Hotel MM 81.4 - 1935

After the 1935 Hurricane.
(Photos courtesy of the Florida Keys Historical Society.)

The guides in those days worked for just a couple of dollars a day. As business was hard to come by, most guides needed to support themselves by doing odd jobs or some other form of day labor. One such guide who was working in the Matecumbe area in the late 20's and 30's was Capt. Billy Smith, who is credited with catching the first bonefish by intention on fly, but that does not come until a bit later in the story.

Early bonefishermen fished with casting rods and direct drive casting reels with braided line. This equipment made casting any distance with any accuracy a great challenge, so a lead egg sinker was added to provide some heft to throw. However, even as early as the 30's, the ORVIS Company and others were trying to produce fly rods that would stand up to the harsh saltwater environment. The motivation to perfect fly casting equipment wasn't driven just by the sporting aspect of fly fishing, people sought to develop the equipment because they knew it was an effective way to deliver bait or a lure at some distance with good accuracy compared to the casting equipment of the day. So it happened that Orvis sent Capt. Billy Smith three, 9 ½ foot, 9 wt. rods to test and on the agreement he report his findings back to them.

By the early and mid-30's there were also guides, such as Leo Johnson operating in the Middle Keys and back country, that were taking baby tarpon on what he called a poor man's fly. A poor man's fly was a bit of feathers on a 2/0 hook with a piece of pork rind trailing behind.

Because of the low horsepower engines of the day (5 to 10 hp) and the length of time it would take to get to favorite angling spots or the backcountry, Leo had a large boat called "Hobo" which he would use to take his anglers in to the backcountry. They would live on board for a few days and fish on his skiff "Tramp" that would be left in the backcountry to save time going back and forth. This is a striking contrast to today's fishing; today we merely hop on a 120 to 200 hp skiff in Key Largo or Islamorada and we can be at Flamingo in 30 to 40 minutes.

Up until then, one of the reasons no one had bothered to pursue bonefish with a fly was that a well-known fly fishing angler of the day who lived in Islamorada had pronounced that it couldn't be done. This angler was George LaBranche, known to be the father of dry fly fishing and introducer of the art of dry fly fishing in North America. George had retired to Islamorada in his later years to enjoy the warm weather and the excellent fishing. Because of his expertise and knowledge of fly fishing his pronouncement that bonefish would not take a fly was accepted as gospel and the fishermen in the Keys at that time didn't even bother to try.

The Salt-Us
Capt. Billy Smith's fly that caught the first bonefish in 1939.

In fact, it was the pursuit of baby tarpon on fly that brought Capt. Smith and his client, angler George Crawford, together in 1938. Mr. Crawford wanted to try for tarpon on fly, so Capt. Billy had tied up some red and white hackle feathers on a 1/0 hook and tipped it with strips of pork rind.

It was on that spring afternoon in 1938 while casting to tarpon that Capt. Billy's angler did in fact hook and land two nice size bonefish. However, as Capt. Billy personally and proudly displayed and weighed them at the A&B Grocery Store (the only commercial scales in the area), George LaBranche happened to be present and declared that they were not legitimate fly catches of record, as the fly hook had been tipped with bait.

An embarrassed and aggravated Capt. Smith went home that evening still convinced in his own mind that the pork rind had been incidental to the catch and that bonefish would in fact take a fly. However, it wasn't until the following year that he tied up another fly, similar but with orange thread on a 1/0 hook with red and yellow hackle and an ostrich feather wing over a squirrel hair body to be used in his future pursuits. He left them sitting on his workbench. (see picture top page) He even named this fly the "Salt-Us".

*Picture of Capt. Billy Smith taken by Irene Pinder in 1939
when he caught the first bonefish on fly.*

Not long after on a calm clear afternoon when he had nothing better to do, Capt. Billy took his home creation fly and his ORVIS Battenkill experimental fly rod and headed off to Little Basin in Islamorada. There he did in fact hook and land a bonefish and even had the good fortune to have a reputable witness who was boating nearby and came to see what was going on. As it turned out, the witness, Mr. Norris, also just happened to be a good friend of one Mr. George LaBranche and could verify Billy's accomplishment.

Capt. Billy Smith continued to guide, tie and sell both jigs and flies until close to age 80 after which he lived in Crystal River, Florida well into his 90's.

It should also be noted that Capt. J. T. Harrod of Miami, one of the early guides working out of Miami, reported that one of his regular anglers, a Colonel L. S. Thompson of Red Bank, New Jersey caught a bonefish on a Royal Coachman fly while fishing for small tarpon in the late 20's.

The sport of taking bonefish on fly developed very slowly during the 40's and early 50's, and there were good reasons for that. People were distracted by the realities of World War II, and by the equipment limitations. However, by the mid-50's, spinning equipment was the standard equipment and with monofilament line an angler could cast a weighted jig a considerable distance with great accuracy. There were a few purists around who were pursuing the sport with fly rods and flies, but in the 50's and even 60's, they were definitely the exception.

A number of these exceptional anglers deserve recognition. One such early bonefish guide of the day was Jimmy Albright. Jimmy was also quite capable and willing to take a client for bonefish on fly. Like most guides of the time he developed his own fly patterns. Jimmy's wife was also an addicted angler, fly tier and guide. They crafted a fly that worked particularly well then and still works well today. It is called the Frankie Belle, named after Jimmy's wife Frankie and her regular angler client, Belle.

The Frankie Belle.

Other legendary guides of the late 1940's and early 1950's include Billy Knowles, Cecil Keith, and Dick Williams all of whom guided for over 60 years.

It is interesting to note that Capt. Albright, Billy Smith and another well-known guide of the day, Johnny Cass, all married sisters. Frankie married Jimmy, Bonnie married Billy, and Beulah married Johnny. The sisters were also accomplished anglers and even guided during the early 40's to supplement their income during the years that their husband's were away in the service for WW II. This was a pursuit they enjoyed as much as their customers and they continued to guide well after the war ended.

Another notable early guide was George Hommell. He started to guide in 1952 and became not only famous for his skills as a guide, but as founder of World Wide Sportsman and in later years for his efforts in guiding for President Bush (41st) on his highly publicized fishing holidays in the Keys. Can you imagine trying to catch a Keys bonefish with a Secret Service boat following and a chopper overhead? Poor guy!

Like George Hommell, Don Bowers was also a guide to Presidents, providing his services over several years to President Hoover who stayed and fished out of the Key Largo Angler's Club. Don also had an opportunity to guide President Eisenhower. Don Bowers, Dick Pinder, Pete Purdue, Tommy Gifford, and Bill Curtis were guiding in the 50's but in the northern Keys and Biscayne Bay. Stu Apte was also guiding during this time, but in the lower Keys. The rod of choice until the mid 50's continued to be a Pfleuger Supreme with a Penn 109 reel, until replaced by Shakespeare and Mitchell spinning equipment.

Early picture of Stu Apte & Ted Williams
(Photo courtesy of Stu Apte)

Pay for a guide in the early 1950's was up to $25 per day, up almost ten-fold increase from the 30's.

The Key Largo Angler's Club was one of the early angling motivated establishments. Opening year around in the mid-30's, it provided service to eastern yachtsman as well as anglers sent down from the Biltmore Hotel in Miami.

In those days, the method of moving a boat across a flat was slightly different than today. The guides would often pole their skiff from the bow where they would spot the fish, cast to it, and then hand the rod to the angler. However, by the late 50's and 60's the spinning rod was dominating and casting became easier and more accurate. The early guides who had fly fishermen on board would pole by standing on the engine cover so that the fly angler could use the bow to manage his line. As you might imagine it didn't take much of this before the idea of a poling platform was hatched. Bill Curtis, an early Biscayne Bay guide, is credited with that development. This unique development brought more than one laugh from fellow guides but they all quickly realized its merit and followed suit.

Poling platform first conceived by legendary guide Bill Curtis.

Interestingly, it was several years later before the angler platform or bow platform was developed. As best I can research, I believe this credit goes to Flip Pallot who put it on board about 1980.

Every modern day Keys angler who gets his one or two bonefish per day pines for the "good ole days". However, even then it was no pushover with 6 to 8 fish being a very good day's work. Legendary guide and angler Stu Apte however did have one day when his husband & wife clients hooked 27 and landed 16 fish. It's been a while since those numbers have happened in the Florida Keys.

The number of anglers in pursuit of bonefish and the number of guides increased rapidly in the 1960's and 1970's. Legendary angler and sportscaster Curt Gowdy and his American Sportsman TV show were regular visitors to the Florida Keys and helped to quickly popularize the pursuit of bonefish and tarpon on fly.

By the 1970's buggy whips (fly rods) were a frequent sight on the flats with the tournament circuit that was evolving offering special recognition and extra points for fly anglers, and there was even a fly only tournament organized by the late 70's.

Bud 'N Mary's and The Lorelei became principal providers of guide services in the Middle and Upper Keys with anglers often staying at Cheeca Lodge and other nearby accommodations and enjoying a fabulous after fishing meal at one of the fine local restaurants like Ziggy's Conch. A day of fishing would now cost you $100 per day and the more popular guides like Hank Brown, George Hommell, Rick Ruoff, Steve Huff, Eddie Wightman, and Joe Lepree being booked from April through June with their regulars one year ahead. In those days fish were often killed for mounting, tournaments, or just settling wagers. A mount could bring the guide $25 to $35 which was a significant part of the day's wages.

There doesn't seem to be good figures on the number of bonefish killed, but by the 70's there were over 5000 tarpon killed per year for tournaments or mounting at that time. Today the legal tarpon kill is down to about 100.

There are no hard facts as to why the Florida Keys fishery experienced such a decline, but it was in the 60's that people fish began to notice the dwindling fish populations. Bill Curtis believes today's visible populations are down by 90% compared to the early 1950's. Don Bowers is a strong believer that the boats that ran the edge of the mangroves day after day in the 60's and 70's looking for square grouper (marijuana bails) were a big part of the negative effect on population. Fortunately, organizations like Bonefish & Tarpon Unlimited are committed to unlocking the puzzle in the hope of providing a remedy. There are many logical suspects but few facts; water pollution, destruction of juvenile habitat, boat traffic, angler pressure, catch mortality, and the list goes on.

Somewhere along this chronology, sport fishermen began to travel to the islands of the Bahamas in pursuit of bonefish. Many of the same fishermen had discovered that although smaller, the bonefish in the Bahamas were a whole lot more numerous and considerably dumber. Local Bahamas fishing guides like Bonefish Willy and Bonefish Bob began to become known from Bimini to Georgetown.

1960's Abaco bonefishing outing.
(Picture courtesy of Frontiers Travel.)

One of the more famous Bahamian guides, Charlie Smith, was namesake of the most popular of all bonefish flies, the "Crazy Charlie". Charlie operated out of Andros Island and could throw a good fly line himself. He knew how to put an angler on numerous pockets of fish. Rupert Leadon and his Andros Island Bonefish Club, Peace & Plenty in Georgetown, and Deep Water Cay on Grand Bahama were the early fishing destination lodges to make a permanent mark in the Bahamas bonefishing popularity.

Tom Davidson with Charlie Smith (namesake of the Crazy Charlie fly)

It was some years later before bonefishing for sport spread to other more far-away locations throughout the world. For example, locations like Christmas Island didn't get going until the mid-70's, and Mexican resorts of the Yucatan began to prosper in the 1980's. The Seychelles, today's popular big fish / big count destination, didn't open until the late 1990's.

By the mid-80's bonefishing was becoming a significant recreation industry in several countries and definitely big business in the Keys, Bahamas, Mexico and others. Sandy Moret had opened his very popular Saltwater Fly Fishing School, which along with ace instructors like Flip Pallot, Stu Apte, and Chico Fernandez are responsible for a significant part of the momentum that replaced spinning rods on the flats with fly rods. Reel Technology also evolved with the Ted Jurassic / Billy Pate and Abel reels evolving to meet the needs of the Florida Keys anglers.

Peace & Plenty
(Photo compliments of Frontiers Travel.)

Fly fishing for bonefish is here to stay and unless someone starts doing it with lasers or holograms, it's hard to see what will stop it or slow it down.

Oh yes, and by the year 2000, you were paying $400 for a days fishing, usually accompanied by a generous tip. We have come a long way from $2 per day.

Tight lines to all of you.

Sandy Moret makes a technical point at his
Florida Keys Fly Fishing School.

CHAPTER II

Equipment

There is so much wonderful equipment to choose from today that it may seem to be more complicated and confusing than it was several years ago. However, most of the alternatives are all good so it is hard to go wrong.

Most bonefish anglers prefer a 7 to 9 weight fly outfit, i.e. combination rod and line.

The first piece of equipment to consider is the rod. To begin with, the higher the number, the stouter or stronger the rod. This means that it takes more force to load or bend the rod and that the rod while straightening out in the casting process will deliver more force to the line. Either the 7, 8 or 9 weights are all quite capable of catching the largest and strongest of bonefish, but there are more subtle advantages to the different weights.

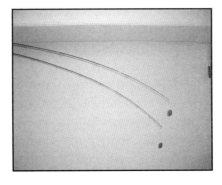

Two fly rods with equal weights suspended from the tip.
The 7 wt. rod (low number rod) deflects further than the 9 wt. rod.

Advantages of a stronger rod:
- More casting power which is helpful on windy days.
- Tires the fish faster and puts less stress on the fish than a longer fight with a lighter rod.
- Better able to turn the fish if you need to guide the fish around obstructions or away from the boat.

Advantages of light rods:
- Slightly easier or less tiring to cast.
- More action and challenge in fighting the fish.

Personally I prefer the heavier rods. Although I am embarrassed to say, I have more than 2 dozen fly rods. I must confess I almost always use my old stand-by a 9 wt. Sage RPLX graphite. This rod is a fairly stiff, quick rod.

There are numerous quality rod manufacturers all of whom make fine products. The better known 7 to 9 wt. rod manufacturers include Sage, Orvis, Loomis, St. Croix, Winston, Redington and Scott. Their rods are quite similar but vary in what is known as the stiffness or quickness of the rod. The slower the rod, the more forgiving it may be to a bad cast stroke. But the trade off is that it is less responsive when you need a little something extra from the rod.

The choice of line also involves a dazzling array of options. Before discussing manufacturers' differences, let's first look at the types of line. There are sinking lines, floating lines, and float lines with sinking tips. Most bonefishermen prefer a floating line as it is much easier to pick up off the water for a re-cast (heaven forbid one should need one), and in most cases as you fish in less than 3 feet of water, the weight of the fly is sufficient to take the fly and leader to the bottom for presentation to the fish.

The next decision is a little more complicated and relates more to the angler's own personal casting-style. This involves the selection of the taper. There are double tapers where the line is symmetrical with an equally shaped taper on each end of the line and usually a more gradual tape than the other alternatives. This line has the advantage of being reversible. For example, when the business end begins to show some wear, you can empty the line from the reel and reverse the ends and load it back on the reel with virtually a new line. The other advantage of the double taper is that it lands softer than the heavier tip lines. This can be a substantial advantage to avoid spooking the fish.

However, in spite of these advantages, the double taper is less popular for bonefishing than some of the forward –loaded tapers. This is because a line with a heavier loading toward the tip has steeper taper which allows one to advance more line with a single false cast and is particularly useful for short, into the wind, casts. These lines include: weight forward, bonefish taper, saltwater taper, and rocket taper to mention a few.

I use a bonefish taper but it is truly a matter of personal choice and your overall success and enjoyment will likely not turn on this decision. My personal recommendation would be to go with a weight forward or bonefish taper that would be identified on the package as:

Example:
8 W F F

8—weight
WF—Weight Forward
F—Floating

Once the line is on your reel, if you have more than one reel (and you will), it becomes hard to remember or distinguish the weight of the line. To overcome this I mark my line with a magic marker. One broad band for 5 and smaller strikes for each single. For example, in Roman numeral concept – one broad band and two narrows mean 7 and so on.

Now we need to pick a brand. There are several of these and in most cases all good. Orvis, Scientific Angler and 3M are probably the most popular. Within each brand they have different choices of line type that relates primarily to the slickness or stiffness of the lines. Some claim to be slicker than others, which means they will advance through the guides with less force; some claim to require less cleaning; some claim to have less memory or less tendency to return to the coiled shape of the reel. There are subtle differences and not a lot will likely turn on your particular choice. I use Orvis Wonderline which is slick and easy to clean; however one negative is that it has a bit of a memory. We will talk more about this is in our "How To" chapter.

When it comes to reels there are even more choices. To begin with, many of the rod manufacturers such as Orvis also have reels. In addition, there are several other very popular names: Abel, Billy Pate, Tibor, Mackenzie Ross, Waterworks, Lawson, and Sea Master.

Before talking about choices, let's first talk about the job the reel has to perform.

- First and obvious, it has to hold or store the line.
- Second and more important, it provides the braking action or the resistance to line advancement that is the pressure control used when fighting the fish. The brake system must be smooth, reliable and fool proof. Bonefish are too hard to catch to risk a break-off for a poor quality or faulty drag.
- There are several key design differences. There is left-hand wind or right-hand wind which is strictly a matter of personal choice as with golf or any other sport.

Then there is the key decision of direct drive or anti-reverse or a combo. Direct drive means that every time the fish pulls line off of the reel, the reel handle turns as well. Anti-reverse reels allow the line to be pulled from the reel without rotating the handle.

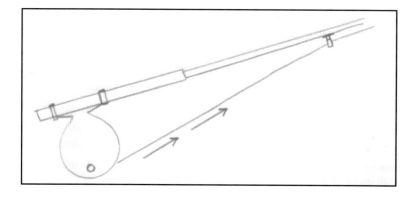

Anti-reverse allows line to be pulled off by
the fish without moving the reel handle.

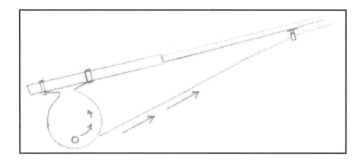

*Direct drive reel: The reel handle rotates
counterclockwise as the fish takes line from the reel.*

Many manufacturers offer both styles. I strongly recommend and personally prefer the anti-reverse as being an easier, less error prone system for the average angler, but hasten to add that many of the pros would disagree with me on this.

There are also some clever hybrids. Several reels like the Billy Pate / Ted Juracsik offer anti-reverse but are designed with an exposed reel rim so that an experienced angler can also apply additional breaking pressure to the line by rubbing the rim of the reel with the palm of the hand (called palming).

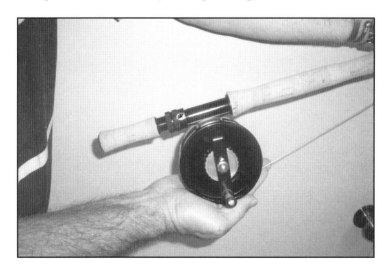

Palming a reel to provide variable braking pressure.

Sea Master, who has made high quality and very high-priced saltwater fly reels for years, makes a reel that is a combo direct drive and anti-reverse. It's an ingenious design. If the angler applies positive pressure to the handle, the reel behaves as a direct drive not letting line advance from the reel. Conversely by releasing the forward rotation pressure on the handle it reverts to an anti-reverse mode allowing line to advance against the preset pressure of the brake without turning the handle.

One of the important advancements in reel design during the last 15 years has been the development of the large arbor reels. Many manufacturers offer both large and small arbor reels. The advantages of a large reel are two-fold. First, every revolution of the reel picks up a longer length of line than a small arbor (i.e. small diameter) reel. This allows the angler to keep up with a bonefish that is charging toward the boat, which happens frequently. The second advantage is that the line has less memory or tendency to want to recoil when it is removed from the reel for casting. In short, I would strongly recommend that someone buying new equipment consider the larger arbor designs as there seems to be very little, if any, negative and several positives.

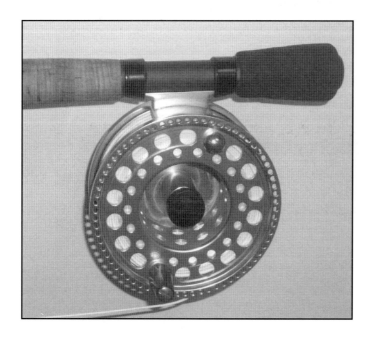

*Large
Arbor
Reel*

While speaking of equipment and line there is one additional piece of equipment that is new on the market that is definitely worth a mention. In fly fishing for bonefish, managing your excess line (or running line) on a windy day, or on any day for that matter, is essential to a successful cast. The general rule is if you don't know where your line is, it is probably where it shouldn't be. Under your foot, around the push pole holder, around the rod holder, or wrapped around your tackle bag.

There are several products that attempt to deal with this problem. They include stripping baskets of various sizes, even ones that strap on your leg (a really tough arrangement), but up until recently I had never found anything I liked very well.

This new solution is a new product called a ***FlyLine Tamer***. (See picture below.) It is about a 3 foot tall cylinder with a weighted bottom for stability. When setting up to fish, you strip your free line into the cylinder and there it stays safe and sound and out of harms way awaiting your big moment.

Like anything in fishing, it's pricey at approximately $150, but on a windy day believe me it is worth twice the price.

It is also very handy at the end of the fishing day to simply stick your gloves, glasses and hat inside the can and carry it off home.

Like many bonefishing and fly fishing enthusiasts I have more rods and reels than I would care to have my wife know about. However, in spite of all these alternatives I usually pick up my old standby rig which is a 9 ft. 9 weight Sage RPL rod with a glass-eyed tip eyelet and a Seamaster reel with a 9 wt. bonefish taper Wonderline. This combination will handle the biggest of bonefish, most permit, and even the occasional small tarpon. It also provides the extra power I like when throwing into the wind or when you are trying for that last few feet of distance.

Chapter III

Boats, Motors & Props

Boats & Motors

No doubt one could write a book about this subject alone, and I have no intention of trying to cover it in that depth nor do I have the knowledge to do so, even if I did have the inclination. However, there are a few basic facts about good bonefish skiffs that I have learned over the years by hard knocks.

In buying a flats boat, one needs to start with and accept the reality that there is no one perfect boat that does it all. On one hand, one type of boat is great for traveling in choppy water at high speed. Another one is very stable for stake out in choppy water for tarpon, but too heavy and noisy for effective stalking of bonefish in calm, shallow water. As this book is focused primarily on bonefish, let's look at the needs from that perspective.

For bonefishing there are several requirements a good boat must measure up to.
- Quietness in the water while being poled.
- Draft.
- Ease of poling (boat weight, free board, etc.)
- Seaworthy and dryness while under power.
- Adequate dry storage.
- And of course, price.

If you assume that catching fish is the principal objective, then other than seaworthiness and safety, quietness becomes a very big factor in boat selection. Water slap noise made by small waves or chop splashing against the sides of the boat, or more likely the underside of the chines. The chine is the front hull or side hull contour that deflects the water out and away from the hull to provide a dryer ride. Regrettably, other than trying a boat first hand, it is hard to get a fix on the noise issue because all manufacturers claim their boats are quiet. In fact, before buying any skiff, spending a day fishing on a similar one is an excellent prerequisite as you will get a firsthand feel not only for noise but comfort, pole-ability, storage capacity, etc.

Second to noise, pole-ability and dry ride are very important factors and these are often a compromise of one for the other.

A lightweight boat (700 lbs. or less) with low freeboard (10" or less) will be a lot easier to maneuver and will pole much easier than one that weighs 1000 lbs. with high freeboard. Most manufacturers will offer a Kevlar fiberglass construction as an option for about $1000 extra. This will take about 100 to 150 lbs. off the hull weight and has proven to be both strong and smooth.

From the first hand experience that I have had, easy to pole boats would include the Dolphin Super Skiff, Hells Bay, Maverick Mirage, and the new Scout Boat Stu Apte Series skiff. In my opinion, boats that don't do well in this category would include the larger Mavericks, Silver King, and Lake & Bay.

Another factor related to pole-ability is the poling platform. Many platforms, in my opinion, are too small and too tall. I prefer my platform no taller than necessary to clear the motor when it is in the tilted position, and it must have good depth (front to back) and width (side to side).

The higher platforms are hard to get up and down on, particularly if you are a bit gray at the temples. Although a high platform gives you a better angle for fish sighting, there is also a point of diminishing return. And remember—it also gives the fish a better look at you. I like the wide, deep platforms because they let me, a non-professional poler, widen my stance for better stability and give me a little more tolerance for a misstep in repositioning my feet. A platform with a raised edge is a plus as you can keep your eyes on fish and can easily feel the edge.

*Cut down poling platform to just clear the engine in
raised position. Also has raised edge to allow poler
to detect edge of platform without looking down.*

While on the subject of platforms, I also prefer a boat with a
front casting platform for the angler. It must not be too high, as you
will be noisier getting up and down on a high one. Also, if it is too
high it is easier for the fish to see you. On the other hand, a plat-
form must be high enough to improve your sight line. The second
benefit of the casting platform is that it allows your fly line to lie
both on the bow deck or on the cockpit floor and away from your
feet. There is nothing more frustrating than when you have found a
worthy target, maneuvered the boat into a perfect position, cranked
up your false cast, and released the line to send the fly to its
appointed mission, only to find that your big left foot is securely
planted on top of the running part of your fly line.

Judging a boat's dryness is not as simple as reading a brochure
or even taking a test ride. There are some boats that handle reason-
ably heavy chop direct on the bow very well, but drown you if the
chop is quartering on the bow or stern. The other problem with a
single test drive is that ones ability to trim the boat with the tabs and
motor is critical to its dryness. Therefore, my suggestion is if prac-
tical, find someone who has a similar boat and who is fairly skilled
at driving it, and get them to give you a test ride varying the angle
of attack to the chop.

If your typical passenger load is two people (you and one other), have a layout where there is a seat on the front side of the center console for one, with the other sitting in the center behind the console. This also improves load distribution and dryness as a bit of side spray can be tolerated and will blow by the stern quarters without hardly touching anyone.

Keep it simple, keep it clean. Most manufacturers are now on top of this one but be sure the forward half of the boat is free of anything that can catch a fly line. If it can catch it, it will and this will almost always at exactly the wrong moment. Cleats, push pole restraints, bow lights, hatch handles and hinges are all potential sources of trouble.

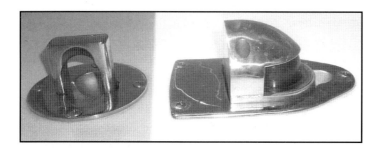

*Cleat &
bow light
in
the use
position.*

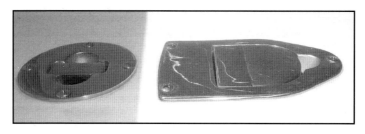

*Cleat &
bow light
stow flat
when **not**
in use.*

If you intend to use an electric motor as a means of propulsion on the flats you have a few basic choices—bow mount, stern mount or trim-tab mount.

From my personal experience, I prefer the bow mount as it is much easier to steer or maneuver the boat with one source of propulsion rather than trying to balance two. However, if you are going to use bow mount, some thought and consideration has to be given to the location and mount style.

There is a new mount system illustrated below that is very effective in leaving your bow clear of obstruction when the motor is not on board. From my experience, it is quite effective in securing the motor and leaves you snag free. It is a bit of a pain to mount and un-mount the motor, but not really a big deal.

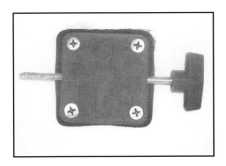 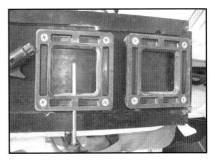

Low profile electric motor mount system leaves only the small snag-free
male mount block on the left picture when motor is not in use.
(Pin would obviously be removed.)

I don't use a trolling motor for bonefishing but I find it very helpful for snook and tarpon. Having said this, the boats that are really good for bones are going to come up a bit short as great tarpon boats.

Using wireless remotes is also very helpful on using your electric motor. There are a couple of remote systems on the market now. One of these is small enough to fit on your belt which is very convenient and practical for those wonderful action moments when you spot several fish, need to cast and move the boat all at the same time.

I personally use a trolling motor with a built-in auto pilot which I love for snook or creek fishing for tarpon. You can give it a heading and adjust the power to match the tide and it will hold you as steady as the best anchor will. It's a testimony to the modern times and the fruits of free trade that you can buy a great electric motor with built-in auto pilot south of $1000.

There are also trolling motors built right into the trim tabs for about $1500. This is a great concept and easier to drop down for use but they do add weight to the back of the boat and increase your overall draft.

Trim Tab mounted electric motors provide lots of thrust, easy steering, and very convenient out of the way storage when not in use.

Before leaving the subject of electric motors, a point should be made about battery location and weight. A good manufacturer or boat yard should know your boat well enough to advise on extra battery location. Normally a bow or console mount to distribute the weight is preferable. One heavy duty extra battery wired to be rechargeable from your boat engine or 110 shore power will usually take care of most needs unless you plan to be a really heavy user of your electric motor between engine starts.

The right engine is a critical part of your boat choice. It also is a balance of weight, power and of course, money. The distances you plan to run between flats and between the dock and the flats will effect this equation in an obvious way. For the smaller, lighter boats like the Dolphin Super Skiff, Hells Bay or Mirage, the 70 to 90 horsepower, 3 cylinder motors are a good choice. They don't over-weight your boat and give you lots of speed unless you really need that extra 4 knots on the top end. The advent of the 4 stroke engine has also changed the game as there are significant advantages of quietness and efficiency, and are a good alternative to consider. The good news is that the reliability of most engines today is excellent and much improved from 15 years ago. Most with reasonable care and respect will give you many seasons of trouble-free boating.

Storage is a very personal matter and the needs will vary widely from person to person. Everyone needs safe, convenient rod storage and convenient storage for safety equipment and tackle. Some people's needs stop there while there are others who like to have the kitchen sink… just in case. I must confess that I tend to be in the latter category.

The one thing that is important to all is that the dry storage be dry. I have had some personal disappointments in this area and I would recommend that you have a clear understanding with the company you are buying the boat from that dry means dry.

Another aspect of a boat to consider is the bait well, as a good functioning bait well is important to most boaters. The well overflow should be designed not to clog with bait or foreign particles. It should also have a good reliable pump, and better yet, a spare or dual pump. I also highly recommend either having a separate live well if space permits (it probably won't) or make your bait well large enough to hold a live bonefish. There are two reasons for this. One reason is that it might come in handy if you plan to be a tournament fisherman. The other reason is to protect your fish from predators. If you fish waters frequented by aggressive sharks it is a good idea to put your played fish in the live well to recuperate and release it 10 to 20 minutes later near some cover. You can also buy bait well pumps that install by snap fit. This makes repair much easier as these items are definitely prone to failure.

One additional option I really like is a steering wheel with a Neckers knob. (See picture below.) This simple little 1940's invention from which it derives its name make it very easy to steer your boat in tight turns while leaving one hand free for other purposes, like adjusting the throttle, etc.

Neckers Knob makes
one hand steering easy.

When it comes to storing your skiff it is highly desirable to get it out of the water when it is not being used, as this helps keep the bottom of the boat clean. There are several ways to accomplish this. One option is to have stand boat lift davits, and another option is to put the boat on the trailer between uses. But, the method I prefer is a floating jet ski dock. These are relatively inexpensive ($3000 to $4000) and are easier than it appears to drive the boat up on to. These docks also have the added advantage of allowing easy access around the boat for both loading and repairs.

*Floating dry docks make an excellent easy
and clean way to store your skiff between uses.*

Props

Selecting the correct prop for your boat can add significantly to your boat's performance. The key variables in prop design and performance are: number of blades, diameter, and pitch. All of these factors relate to affecting the transfer of the rotating power (torque) from your engine power shaft into linear motion of your skiff (normal forward).

The size of the prop is measured not by the diameter of the prop but by the circumference of the circle defined by the out edge of the prop's blades. For skiffs this is normally between about 12 to 15 inches. The larger the prop the better the grip on the water at low speed. This gives better fuel efficiency at low speed, and better hole shot power.

Pitch relates to the shape and depth of the blade shape and is measured by the theoretical distance the prop would move in one rotation if there was a perfect (zero slippage) relationship between the prop and the water. Again, for skiff's the standard pitch numbers would be 15 to 25 inches. At a given engine RPM, the higher the pitch the faster the boat will go at that RPM. This seems simple enough, and it might lead one to believe that simply with bigger pitch, a skiff will have higher speed. Regrettably this is only true to a point. As the pitch increases, the maximum RPM the engine is capable of turning (i.e. top end) is reduced. Therefore, like most things on boats, it is a compromise situation. If you use your boat a lot by yourself without a lot of fuel weight, you can probably enhance performance by getting a higher than standard or factory delivered pitch and vice versa.

The numbers of blades also has an impact on performance. Typically, a 4 blade prop at a given diameter will give you a better hole shot than the same diameter in a 3 blade design, but you will give up top end performance as a trade off. On the other hand, one can often enhance performance out of the hole and top end by using a 4 blade at a slightly smaller diameter than a standard 3 blade.

Props generally are made in either stainless steel or aluminum. The aluminum props are less expensive but are not recommended for shallow water use as thy just don't hold up to the abrasion or bumps that a typical skiff boat experiences. Regrettably, the stainless steel props cost more, but they are worth it in the long run. However, it is a good idea to keep that stock aluminum prop as your back up prop.

To purchase or specify a prop, they are defined by two numbers, i.e. 15 x 22, which is a prop with a 15" circumference and a 22" pitch. The number of blades is somewhat obvious.

There you have it. More than you ever wanted to know about props.

CHAPTER IV

Fly Casting

I don't profess to be a world-class fly caster, and this chapter won't attempt to teach basic fly casting. However, I have been throwing a fly line for 50 plus years (mostly perfecting my bad habits) and I have learned a few techniques that are useful in bonefishing.

We have already discussed in the equipment chapter (no. 2), that most bonefisherman use a 7 to 9 weight rod with a matching line with some sort of weight forward bias, such as weight forward, or bonefish taper, or saltwater taper. Rods of these weights are serious weapons and can cast a good length of line in a variety of wind conditions. Using a line with the weight biased forward allows one to load the rod on the back cast with a shorter amount of line and thus reduces the amount of false casting that is required to throw a given length of line. As we will discuss, this can be critical in making a timely and stealth cast to a cruising or feeding bonefish.

One bit of cast technique that is essential to be effective at bonefish is the double haul or at least the single haul. For those that know these terms but not the techniques, it is really not as difficult or as complicated as one may have been led to fear. The reason we need to have this technique is many-fold, but the two main reasons in my mind are: Once again it allows us to load the rod with a smaller amount of line and secondly, it gives us much more control of the fly line which can translate into both length and accuracy.

Before you actually start casting, either in our mind or on the water, the first thing you need to do is strip the approximate amount of line off the reel that you feel maybe required to make your anticipated cast. The most effective way to do this is to both pull the line out to a full arms length and count the number of arm length strips that is appropriate for you. i.e. 12, 15, 18, etc. Another obvious solution to this need is to mark your line at the appropriate length with a magic marker or similar device.

OK, we now have a pile of line at our feet which you will note is quite curly. The tendency to curl is called the memory of the lines desire to go back to its previous position of being wound tightly on the reel. To offset this, each time we set up we should stretch the line by pulling through our hands to an arms length, then clamp down on it with both fists, and finally the fists in opposite directions to stretch the line.

Author illustrates stretching the fly line to remove
the cold set curl from the line from being stored on the reel.

By stretching the line, we are straightening the line, which will allow it to flow through the rod eyelets with less resistance.

And now for the double haul. The easiest way I have found to learn this casting technique is to stand sideways to the direction of the cast, so that you can see both your back cast and your forward cast. Try a regular cast or two in this position and you will see that you are able to watch your line flying backwards on the back cast, making it very easy to begin the forward cast just as the line straightens out and begins to bend the rod backwards.

Standing sideways and casting for practice allows a beginner to easily see how the line moves and when to begin the forward motion.

The concept of the haul is to use your left hand to pull on the fly line to create additional loading on the rod tip (stored energy) which will be given back to the line in forward or backward momentum as the rod unloads or straightens back to the neutral position. It is important to note that this set up is for a right-handed caster.

Let's view loading from a more practical or intuitive way. If we had a very, very stiff (non-flexible) material for the rod, we could wave the line back and forth, but it would be much more difficult to build the sustained force on the line that we are looking for to pull the line forward, and create sufficient momentum to drag the line in reverse, or to drag the running line through the eyelets and out the rod tip.

Conversely with a material like a graphite fiberglass combination, it is rigid but bendable, we are able to cause it to flex with the casting motion and in flexing we cause it to store energy which will be given back to the line as it unflexes or straightens.

The pick up haul or the Stage (1) haul applied to the back cast is very effective and very easy. To effect it, you simply slide your left hand up the fly line toward the first eyelet on the rod. You do this at the moment you are about to begin the backward movement of the rod (back cast) or the point where the rod begins to pick the line up from the water. As you begin to move the rod backwards (i.e. create the back cast) you simultaneously pull down on the line or pull it away from the rod. By so doing, you will readily feel the additional loading or flex it creates in the rod, and consequently, the force with which it will propel the line in the backward direction when it straightens out.

STAGE I OF BACKCAST HAUL

*Slide hand up
the line toward the
first rod eyelet
to begin the pick up
or backcast.*

Hand pulls the line down during the backcast to create additional loading.

Practice this a few times to get the feel of it. It is really not very difficult. This is also very helpful in breaking the line away from the water and getting the entire casting motion started.

Now let's turn to the more exciting part of the haul technique, the Stage (2) or the forward haul. Forget all about the first stage or pick up haul for the moment. Stand sideways and make a back cast but this time as the back cast unfolds, let your left hand moved up the fly line near the first eyelet again. Now just as you are starting forward with your cast, give a downward pull on the fly line like we did in the Stage (1) haul. It does not need to be huge yank; just a good steady pull will suffice.

STAGE II OF FORWARD CAST HAUL

Forward cast begins with the left hand higher on the line.

The line is gently pulled down with the left hand during the forward cast to create additional loading and is then released as the line advances.

You will probably notice that the line moves with much more authority in the forward cast and has considerably more shooting momentum as the rod returns to the straight or natural position.

Practice this a few times until you get comfortable with it. Learning the forward haul is paramount to good casting even if you never conquer the step of combining Stage 1 and Stage 2. Once you learn the Stage 2 haul you will subconsciously use it on all your casts, even with a 3 weight rod in a trout stream, as it just improves the overall line control by an order of magnitude.

Now comes the fun, combining Stage 1 and Stage 2. It really isn't that hard, it's just that it's like rubbing your stomach while patting your head. We just need to start by doing stage 1 and as the line is sliding through our hand and going out the back cast, we move our left hand forward with the line so it is in a position to pull the line down again on the forward stroke.

However, for this moment if you have mastered stage 2—the forward haul—you can catch lots of fish. But the little additional momentum that the forward haul provides can be a huge help in making accurate and authoritative casts.

In casting the wind can be your friend.

However, before discussing the wind and how to use it, there is one more casting basic we should discuss and that is the matter of open loop or tight loop. With a big firm bonefish rod and a relatively stiff wrist one can throw a very tight parallel cast.

*Stiff wrist during
forward cast
to maintain tight
loop.*

Conversely by flexing the wrist in the early stage of the forward cast, the loop will open considerably.

*Cocked or loose
wrist to create
open loop.*

A tight loop has the advantage of less wind resistance as the line (and fly) is in effect drafting on itself as it moves through the cast, much in the same way two-speed bikes do or two race cars do.

In casting, the wind can often work against you, but as stated earlier, in many cases the wind can be your friend. Let's first deal with a tail wind as it is easy to see how that might work in your favor. As this wind will restrict your back cast, you need to start with a big bold stage 1 haul on the back cast. If you have executed this well, the front cast will be easy, as the wind will be working with you to carry the line forward.

Unless you are really trying to ride the wind in the shooting phase of the cast for an extra long cast, you are better off keeping our tight loop (stiff wrist cast) so that you control the line and deliver it to its desired target on schedule. However, in this condition if you are trying to ride the wind for an exceptionally long cast, you should make a good forward haul on the forward cast but open your loop up a little (flex our wrist) to allow the wind more line to push against in the shooting phase of the cast.

With the wind quartering from the rear, or directly off to your side, or even quartering from the front, you should still be able to execute very effectively as the conditions should not affect your length all that much, but it does introduce two other elements we need to deal with.

The first of these is side drift of the line which will obviously want to go left when the wind is from our right and vise versa. Here again, the tighter your loop the less the affect will be, but it will exist, particularly on a long cast or shoot. In this case, your instincts and experience are the best guide on how much, but one thing you can do is "sight in" so to speak. That is when you find yourself turning into such conditions, make a trial cast to gauge the effect.

However, when these quartering or a beam winds are coming from our right side, you have an additional challenge. That is, the wind will have a tendency to blow your fly line towards the caster's head, and if you have ever been hit by a lead eyed Crazy Charlie traveling at high speed, you will probably still remember it. One easy way to avoid this is to tilt the rod away from your body to move the path of the line further from your cranium. You need to remember that the line follows the rod tip, so you still need to move the rod tip in a straight path toward your wind adjusted target. If you make a curved motion with the rod tip, you have introduced a whole new sct of problems we don't even want to discuss.

While we are dealing with the wind quartering or coming from our right side, it is also a good time to introduce the concept of the backhand cast. This can be a very useful technique in a variety of circumstances. This cast is affected by making a false cast directly away from the target, which now becomes a down wind cast and then back cast the line to the real target. It sounds complicated but it is really very easy. Try it a few times. As the man says, "Try it, you will like it".

Now we come to the cast everyone dreads and avoids—the into the wind cast. I won't say that it doesn't present problems because it does, but it is not as bad as most believe it to be if you follow a few basic rules. First of all, a powerful back cast (the key to most good casts) is less important here as the wind will very definitely come to your aid on that phase. On the forward cast you need to focus on a stiff wrist for a nice tight loop and a nice steady forward motion with the rod, and a nice steady forward haul. Most casts into the wind are screwed up by trying to force the cast, or casting too hard or too fast. If you force yourself to make a few easy steady casts into the wind with a sustained steady forward haul to help the line turn over at the end of the cast (rather than blow back toward the angler), you will be surprised how well you will do.

One other aspect of casting that is critical to making a successful bonefish hookup is to be able to make the cast with as few false casts as possible. This means you should be able to cast at the sighted fish with no false casts, one false cast, or at the very, very maximum two fast casts. This is critical because each time you wave that big long stick and line around, (and our own arms for that matter), there is a good chance it will catch the eye of the fish you are stalking and he is gone. Using no false cast or only one false cast is not as hard as it sounds.

All successful casts start with the set up. I carry about 20 feet of line beyond the tip of the rod with the fly in my left hand when I am waiting for a target opportunity. This amount of line I can control, keeping it out from under the boat, etc., but can also bring it in one motion into a strong enough back cast to be able to advance some additional line by the line pull on the back cast. If it is a relatively short cast that is required, by using a single forward haul on my forward cast with no false cast, I can advance a considerable amount of line, and you should be able to do so as well. Give it a try.

If a longer cast is required, make one false cast advancing line on the forward and backward false cast, now make your delivery forward cast with a forward haul, once again not only to provide cast length but to provide line control, and turn the leader over to complete the cast.

Most freshwater fly fisherman are used to and are more comfortable making several false casts, until they have most of the line length they want in the arc. This just isn't required and will significantly reduce your chance of success.

A false cast is a little bit like a golf practice swing in that it is usually a better stroke than your actual delivery stroke. That's because like a golf swing, we try to put a little something extra on the for real one. Try this exercise working with a friend. Start false casting numerous casts with about the amount of line you would have out on your first false cast, but keep that amount of line constant and continue to false cast back and forth with a modest forward haul on each cast. It will actually feel really good. Then at a moment unknown to you, ask your friend to say release when you are in mid forward cast and you just let go—no extra push with the rod, no extra pull on the line. You will be amazed at what a nice and long cast you will make. With this confidence, you are now ready to try again the one false cast and zero false cast delivery.

Before you go fishing, be sure you are also comfortable with a good old fashioned roll cast from the casting platform. This can be a very effective cast particularly if the target fish has not seen or has ignored your original cast. You can often pick up the line and fly in roll cast fashion if you don't have too much line out. You are usually able to reposition the fly with reasonable accuracy and less commotion than if you attempt a full back cast and forward cast.

A final tip is that fly line casts a lot easier when it is clean. Most of us know to clean our line at the end of a day of saltwater fishing. For this I prefer a single fresh water rinse and wipe down with a cloth with no lubricant or detergent. However, I also learned a good trick from Chico Fernandez, and that is to clean my line with a small polyurethane pad (made by Scientific Anglers). I clean my line with this pad with nothing on it every time I wind in. Try it, it will improve your casting results.

Good luck and good fishing.

CHAPTER V

Bonefish Fly Favorites

Since Capt. Billy Smith intentionally caught the first bonefish on fly in 1939 at Little Basin in Islamorada, there has been a geometric escalation of man's effort to effectively imitate the bonefish's favorite foods.

It actually all started a year earlier when Billy had taken a bonefish by accident using a 1/0 hook with red and white hackle feathers with a strip of pork rind attached. The combo bait/fly was known as a poor man's fly by its developer Leo Johnson, an early Keys guide. As a result of the experience, Capt. Billy's initial bonefish fly, illustrated below, was an attempt to imitate the effect of the combo bait/fly, the Salt-Us.

One of Billy's favorite fly materials was ostrich feathers. He was partial to this medium as he felt is would ebb and flow in the tidal current. He also believed that with a slight line movement, he could create both a real look and an eye catching action to attract the fish. The Salt-Us was a simple but effective streamer-style fly that should work even today. It had red and yellow hackles, and ostrich feather wings over an orange thread wrapped 1/0 hook.

The purpose of the fly is to imitate the appearance of food in the eyes and mind of the bonefish. These food sources are generally believed to be toad fish and other small fish / minnows, shrimp and crabs. Similar to the lesson illustrated by such trout flies as the Stimulator and Royal Wulff, a fly doesn't need to look exactly like a particular food, it just needs to look like it could be food.

The Salt-Us

Capt. Bill Smith's First Bonefish Fly.

Thread: Red-orange
Wing: Light Ostrich over red squirrel tail
Hackle: Red and yellow saddle palmered

Capt. Billy also developed a second fly, called the Tim-rip, with which he had great success. It was the same as the Salt-Us except that it used an orange ostrich wing. It is so named because "Tim-rip" was how Capt. Billy spelled permit backwards. Generally, he found a bit of success hooking them with this color variation.

Another very early enduring fly was the Frankie Belle, developed by Jimmie Albright and named after his fishing guide, partner and wife, Frankie, and her regular fishing partner, Belle Mathers.

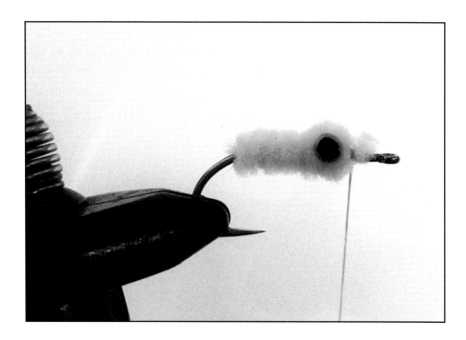

The Frankie Belle

Thread: Chartreuse
Eyes: Yellow with black pupil
Body: Lime chenille
Wing: White calf tail, tied-up style
Overwing: Grizzly Hackle Tips
Note: One of the first patterns to utilize grizzly hackle tips in the wing.

These flies and adaptations of them prevailed until well-known fisherman Bob Navheim developed the Crazy Charlie while fishing with renowned early Bahamian guide Charles Smith in the 70's. The fly was originally called the Nasty Charlie because when Navheim showed the fly to Charlie for his critique, Charlie said, "That is one nasty fly." However, the name Crazy Charlie was used in the Orvis catalog which offered it for commercial sale on large scale, and that name soon stuck. There have been many adaptations of the fly from its inception. A skinned down version of it, the Christmas Island Sparce, is the dominate choice in Christmas Island. Similarly, McVay's Gotcha version of the Charlie is the fly of choice in many waters, especially in the Bahamas, the Charlie's original home. One of the special and important features of the Charlie is its weight distribution, which causes it to land on the bottom with the hook loop up.

Crazy Charlie

Thread: White
Eyes: Painted lead
Tail: White hackle tip
Body: Silver Mylar tinsel
Wing: Several white hackle tips

Gotcha

Thread: *Florescent Orange*
Eyes: *Painted Lead*
Tail: *Pearl Mylar Tubing*
Body: *Pearl Magic Braid*
Wing: *Craft Fur*
Topping: *Few strands of pearl crystal flash*

Several of the many adaptations of the Crazy Charlie
including the Gotcha, Christmas Island Sparce, etc.

Next to appear on the scene were the epoxy head flies which were very popular in the late 1970's and early 1980's. They were easy to make, cast reasonably well, and were fairly durable. Many fishermen stick by them to this day.

Epoxy Fly

The original Epoxy Fly was called the M.O.E. (mother of epoxy) and was
tied by Harry Spears of Islamorada. It is simply a tail of feather, fur or
marabou with plastic eyes and a body shaped out of epoxy.

In designing an effective fly, one must produce a pattern that when in the water, looks like food to the bonefish. However, it must also be castable. The best fly in the world that lands 4 feet behind its intended target will be of little use.

The fly must be compact enough to avoid sailing but fluffy enough and balanced enough to land softly. It's obviously a game of compromises. The weighting of the fly is also critical, and one usually wants to have their favorite pattern in a variety of sizes and weights. Obviously, a heavier fly will sink faster and hold position better in the current. Regrettably, it will also cause a bit more commotion on landing and increase the chance of spooking the fish. I personally prefer to error a bit on the heavy side if I am fishing in more than 13 or 14 inches of water. Not that tailing fish in super skinny water aren't fun to cast to, because they are very exciting, but it's also very difficult to successfully execute a hook up, as these fish are extremely spooky in shallow water and much more sensitive to boat noises and fly splash.

The McCrab

Thread: Brown
Eyes: Lead
Tail: Tan Marabou with a pair of splayed brown hackle topped with a few strands of crystal flash.
Body: Stacked and trimmed deer body hair.
Legs: Knotted rubber epoxied on top with a pair of burnt mono eyes.

The crab patterns began to evolve in the early 1980's. Tom McQuag's McCrab being one of the early and better known patterns. These flies were especially popular for permit fishing; to the extent any fly is effective in catching permit.

By coincidence, a group of friends and I happened to be in camp at Casa Blanca Lodge in Mexico when Tom, in camp with his son, caught his own first permit with his by then well-known McCrab.

The McCrab soon gave way to a variety of other crab patterns that tended to be a bit easier to throw. These soon evolved to more abstract versions of the crab in a series of crossover patterns that could be a crab, shrimp, or something else. The Merkin is one of the better known of this family of flies and is the one we have elected to illustrate. Ironically, this fly gets its name from an artificial hair piece used to cover a woman's private parts. This fly was developed by active angler and tier Del Brown and named by Steve Huff.

Merkin

Merkin

Thread: Chartreuse
Eyes: Heavy Lead Dumbbells
Tail: Few strands of crystal flash with a pair of splayed cree hackle feathers.
Body: Alternating light and dark brown sparkle yarn.
Legs: Four white rubber legs with red tips.

Another distinctive pattern worthy of note is the Puff. It is usually tied in pink or tan, and can come with or without rubber legs. However, I believe the original pattern was pink with no legs for the Bahamas. Personally, I have had good luck with the tan and legged version. This is a very popular fly in many parts of the Bahamas.

The Puff

Thread: Pink
Eyes: Bead Chain
Wing: Sparse white calf
tail tied up style
Overwing: Two grizzly
hackle tips
Head: Medium pink
chenille wrapped figure
eight around the eyes.

The next fly illustrated is one developed by my friend and trusted personal captain / guide, Steve Venini. I must add a special thank you to Steve not only for suffering through my many unsuccessful casts and usual excuses of guide's error, but also for his help in tying all of the flies used in the illustrations in this chapter. Steve is an excellent tier and developer. Steve's recent iteration that we would like to share with you is the Venini Jackcrabit. This fly, tied with a touch of rabbit fur, has proven very effective for the two of us, and we pass it along to you in the hope you will find it similarly successful.

The Venini Jackcrabit

Thread: Florescent orange
Eyes: Black beadchain
Body: Orange chenille
Legs: Three orange rubber legs
Wing: Natural rabbit strip pierced and pulled over hook point
leaving ¼ inch overhang to form tail.
Overwing: Three or four strands of dark orange crystal flash.
Weedguard: 20 lb. mason [I put weedguards on all bonefish flies. It is much
easier to cut them off later than wish you had them when you need them.]
NOTE: This is a wilder version of Steve Bailey's Bonefish Bunny.

One additional fly developed by Steve during the time this book was being written, is one we call Phyllis Diller for obvious reasons. It's a dandy and casts and works well in the Florida Keys. It is a variation of the Puff fly.

Phyllis Diller Fly

Thread: Florescent Green
Eyes: Painted Red with Black Pupil
Wing: Lime crystal flash over red squirrel tail
with a pair of splayed grizzly hackle tips
Body: Green Mylar chenille

CHAPTER VI

Where to Fish

The following are the better known and more popular locations:

Bahamas
Christmas Island, Kiribati
Ascension Bay, Mexico
Central America
Venezuela
Seychelles
Florida Keys USA

The Bahamas are one of the oldest known organized bonefish destinations starting with freelance guides like Bonefish Willie and Charlie Smith in the waters off Bimini and the other locations easily accessed from Florida. In recent years the number of camp locations has proliferated dramatically. I will not attempt to list them all, but the following is a list of camps and locations that are known to me, most of which I have frequented and know a bit about the facilities and fishing. However, I hasten to add that I do not claim to be an expert in the Bahamas.

Bimini / Cat Cay
Numerous freelance guides offering day fishing.
Fish are reasonably accessed on the white sand flats.
The fish tend to be small.
Contact Bimini Big Game Resort & Marina for a place to make private guide contacts.

Andros

Has a number of organized camps and guides. The fish are reasonably plentiful in various bights and on the western side between the north and middle bights the fish are also very large.

> **Rupert Leadon's Andros Island Bonefishing Club** was one of the earlier camps and although the guides and fishing are generally good, it does have the disadvantage of some long boat rides. Also in recent years the quality of the rooms has deteriorated and cuisine tends to favor heavy fried Bahamian style cooking (or at least did in 2001).

> **The Mangrove Cay camp** is one of the new camps located right in the middle bight at Moxey Creek. The guide quality is good and the fishing goes from very good to not so good depending on the weather. They also have reasonable access (a 30 minute plus boat ride) to the big fish on the west side of Andros. The camp is owned by Liz Bain and Shackelton and is very well managed by Liz. The rooms are new and excellent quality, and the food prepared by Chef Ike is very good.

Mangrove Cay Main Lodge

Liz Bain, the very competent manager at Mangrove Cay and a panorama of the very comfortable living units.

Comfortable dock and loading facilities.

The boats at Mangrove are new and have lots of speed.

Mangrove Cay Lodge and guides participate in a bonefish research project with the University of Miami and BTU.

Kamalame Cay is located near the village of Staniard Creek which is separated by Andros by an inlet, and is owned and operated by the very interesting and colorful Brian Hew. Their principal fishing grounds are the jolters, which is an area known to hold lots of fish. The fish tend to be a bit on the small side and the guides tend to take a very disciplined lunch breaks mid-day regardless of what's going on with the tide. The biggest negative is that it is about a 50 minute truck ride to get from camp to the boats.

The rooms are excellent as is the food and service.

Pictures of Lodge units at Kamalame Cay.
(Pictures courtesy of Frontiers.)

Drug runner plane abandoned near the Kamalame camp fishing area.

*A well recognized fishing expression of endearment
from one of my fellow Kamalame Cay fisherman.*

Abacos

<u>Nettie's Abaco Barefoot Beach Resort</u>—It's been a few years
since I have been there but just meeting Nettie Symonette
is worth the trip. She is a most colorful personality with a
flare for the dramatic. The camp compound includes a
recreated early Bahamian village created by Nettie and
what donations she can scare up from others. The compound
is also a bit of a menagerie of exotic animals including var-
ious waterfowl and even peacocks.

The rooms are comfortable and clean and the food is good.

Nettie,
the Grand Dame
of Barefoot Beach.
(Photo courtesy of
Frontiers Travel)

The lodge living
units
at Barefoot Beach.
(Photo courtesy of
Frontiers Travel)

My experience with their fishing is that it is not bad but the fish tend to be small. There are also freelance day guides who are available in several locations including Boat Harbor and Marsh Harbor.

Grand Bahamas

Is home to several good operations.

<u>Deep Water Cay</u> is located at the east end of the island and is one of the oldest and best known of the Bahamas bonefish camps. The ownership of the camp has changed hands a few times over the years and is now part of its own resort community development with lots and homes for sale as well as the camp facilities to rent.

The original cabin units at Deep Water Cay.

(Photos courtesy of Frontiers Travel)

The new lodge dining room at Deep Water Cay.

The camp has access to reasonably good fishing with some larger fish and was made famous by guide Dave Pinder Sr. and his sons. The former has now retired and the sons have mostly moved on to sell their talents to higher bidders.

Author with Chico Fernandez and a group of Ocean Reef buddies on the veranda at Deep Water Cay.

The camp does have a current generation of competent guides who are at your service. They have a bit of a union mentality, but are very capable.

The rooms are good and well maintained with serviceable buildings where 3 or 4 bedrooms share a living room / sitting area which is nice for small groups traveling together.

North Riding Point is located part way along the east side of the island and depending on the wind conditions, either has very close access to good flats or a long way to go. It operates as a private club with the members getting first pick on the dates.

The guides are competent and well outfitted with quality boats and equipment. The fishing, like Deep Water Cay, can be quite good with some reasonable size fish. The rooms and facilities are very good, as is the food.

Pelican Bay is a bit unusual as a fishing operation as it is one of the few bonefish outfitters and locations that offer a night life. It is a virtual camp that operates out of the hotel in Port Lucaya. Fishermen are on their own for dinner but you are within walking distance of many fine restaurants.

Author and a group of friends outside the hotel at Pelican Bay.
We were one of the early groups to visit the Pelican Bay operation.

The operation originally started when the Pinder boys were enticed away from Deep Water Cay with money and the prospect of town living. The guide situation has changed a bit since those early days and I am no longer personally current on the skill levels available there.

Other Bahamas

As indicated, there are numerous other bonefish locations in the islands including many good day fishing options in the Berry Islands and the further out islands like Stanical, Exuma, etc.

Christmas Island

Is part of the Republic of Kiribati and is well known for two things. It was a UK atomic bomb testing base until the 1960's and it was during this period that the plentiful presence of bonefish was detected. Since 1973 it is best known as a bonefish destination. This destination was basically developed by Frontiers, the sporting / travel agents who worked with the local government to offer accommodations, fishing, and air service out from Honolulu to Christmas Island.

The original flight services were provided by an old 4-engine Electra turbo prop that took about 4+ hours to make the flight from Honolulu and made one trip per week, which were basically the 30 odd fishermen that the camp accommodates coming and going. This service was interrupted from time to time over the years for a variety of reasons. During these periods fishing was basically not available unless you had your own plane.

One of the many beautiful flats surrounding Christmas Island.

When the British occupied the island they built a living compound for their use, which resembles an early Howard Johnson style motel, but with not very good food. After the British departure this was operated as a hotel named the Captain Cook Hotel. In recent years they have added a number of 2-bedroom thatched roof cabins that are much more appealing to the eye, but the food hasn't changed much. In spite of this, there has been a steady stream of fishermen in pursuit of what is normally a plentiful supply of bonefish.

Thatched roof cottages are a more recent addition to the housing units.

*The outrigger style motor sailors use to
transport anglers and guides to the flats.*

A skinned-down version of a Crazy Charlie fly, known as the Christmas Island Sparce, is the order of the day and works very well.

With its 30 plus fisherman daily, Captain Cook has a large guide staff, all of which have good eyes and can put you on fish. A couple of the guides soon distinguished themselves from the pack, and now operate as private agents who are booked privately. These are Big Eddie and Moanna. These guides are both excellent and specialize a bit in Trevally fishing (particularly Big Eddie).

The bonefishing is still good today and not that much different from the early days, you just drive a bit further or boat a bit further around the islands, rather than fishing right out the front door so to speak. The big change is that in the early days, Trevally was plentiful and very aggressive in taking a pepper-type fly, if it was stripped in front of them. These guys were big and powerful and put up one hell of a fight. I have a friend and fishing buddy, Joel Shepherd, who in the mid 1970's, claims to have hooked up with a big one while fishing on a sand flat, but while waist high water.

Joel Shepherd, fishing friend of the author, was a regular early day visitor to Christmas Island.

Between the power of the fish and the buoyancy of the water, the fish pulled with Joel bouncing on his heel from one side of the flat to the other. Unfortunately, in the early days fishermen filleted the Trevally and hauled them back home by the cooler full. As a result, there are far fewer of them and they are much harder to catch. Having said that, the picture below is a nice one taken on our trip in 1999 and features a 68 lb. fish caught by a friend, Bill Wheeler who owns and operates a great trout fishing lodge; The Elk Creek Lodge outside of Meeker, Colorado.

Wheeler and Moanna with Bill's trophy trevally.

Christmas Island guide with a good fighting, good eating fish called Sweet Lips.

Davidson with a small trevally.

*Son John
with typical
Christmas
Island
bonefish.*

Fishing buddy Russ Fisher admiring a New Caledonia catch.

While in the area of places far from the North American shores, there has been a lot of effort to start destination bonefishing in <u>New Caledonia</u>, located three hours flight north of New Zealand. The area is beautiful with tall hills and beautiful flats but it has very strong tide currents requiring very heavy flies and there aren't a lot of fish, but it is reported to have some very large fish.

Midway

Midway has also been explored but with only limited success, and has never really become fully operational as a packaged trip.

Mexico

One of the more accessible and popular destinations for bonefishing is the Cancun, Ascension Bay area of Mexico's Yucatan Peninsula.

The two best know camps in this area are **Casa Blanca** and **Boca Paila**.

Both have been in operation for many years and both have large expanses of sand flats and mangrove flats.

> **Casa Blanca** is accessed by a short puddle jumper flight out of Cancun. The camp is not surprisingly a series of white buildings located inside the reef in a beautiful lagoon.

Picture of Casa Blanca camp as you arrive
by boat from the private airstrip.

The camp buildings are simple but clean and well kept, and the food is very fresh and good. Often you eat fish taken on the reef that very day.

It is a good place for beginners, as the fish although small, are reasonably plentiful including a reasonable supply of small permit.

One of the more reliable spots in the area to produce bone-fish hook-ups is an area known as Tres Maria.

Seychelles

The Seychelles is currently the hottest new bonefish ground offering excellent fishing and facilities. For openers, the Seychelles are beautiful and the areas you fish are flats reached by boats from Alphonse Island.

The Seychelles are accessed by plane from Paris, London or Frankfort to Mahe, the capital of the Seychelles Islands, and then a short puddle jump flight by King Air or Caravan over to Alphonse. The facilities awaiting you at Alphonse are right out of Hideaway Reports great small resorts of the World section. There is a beautiful open air style central lodge / dining room building surrounded by approximately 40 very picturesque free-standing bungalows.

Aerial photo of St. Francois Atoll near Alphonse Island.
(Photo courtesy of Frontiers Travel.)

Alphonse Island Bungalow

The author and the first group of 12 to occupy US Fly and Tam Tam Seychelles camps simultaneously.

Alphonse open air dining room.

The food is good, the service is great, but even better is that the fishing is off the charts. Lots of big strong fish.

Seychelles bonefishing was discovered by an English dive charter operator, Martin Lewis and his wife, who would do contract dive charters in the area. Martin is a self-styled marine biologist who was quick to recognize the potential of the plentiful bonefish he discovered when exploring the area. The Seychelles bonefish are a different species from those found in North America and Central America.

As it can get quite windy in the area, Martin used his catamaran yacht, Tam Tam, as a mother ship to ferry anglers to and from the flats.

Martin Lewis' Tam Tam that is used to take anglers to the St. Francois Lagoon.

As the word spread, anglers began to arrive in the area. The Seychelles government was quick to recognize the need for controls and licensed Martin for a 6 rod operation and a new outfitter, Chris Poncon for 6 rods. Chris, with his U.S. Fly operation, took a slightly different approach to the fish access problem, using a modern center console cutter to take his anglers and South African guides out to bonefish skiffs that were already at the flats location.

US Fly trans-portation boat.

The area you fish, St. Francois Lagoon, is relatively small and when both camps are at full capacity of 6 rods each, elbow room is at a premium. On more than one occasion, I tried to convince both Martin and Chris they would be better to raise the price and cut back to 4 rods each with 1 guide per angler.

Fishing buddy Dick Farmer and the author showing off some of the many nice fish taken on St. Francois Lagoon flats.

The fishing on these flats is really superb. During the tide flow, from mid-rise to late-fall, there is scarcely a time when you don't have a target in sight. Even better, the fish here seem to be hotter than the North American fish, giving a longer fight with more fight left at the end. The first time we were there, our group of 12 anglers broke 10 rods with one of these experienced anglers breaking four.

The flats are also populated by an abundance of fairly good size sharks, so one needs to be mindful of these when releasing fish and it is best to stay out of water that is over mid-thigh deep.

The tides here are unusual and don't seem to follow the normal tide cycle. The lows tend to stay low for several hours. During the low tide periods, the bonefishing goes quiet. During these periods one can chase Trevally or hike across the flats (30 minute walk) to an area known as the wreck because of its obvious landmark of a rusted out ship hull. At the wreck one can cast to bonefish and Trevally that work the surf.

Fishing buddy Roe Stamps fishing the surf at the wreck at low tide gets cut off on the way in.

Since 2003, there is another big new game in town; milk fish. This is a totally different family of fish than bonefish and they are strictly vegetarian. However, they are plentiful and strong. When I was first there in 2000, we tried unsuccessfully to catch them in a variety of ways. Fellow angler Russ Fisher tried to tie a fly that looked like a grass shoot. It turns out Russ was on the right track, and a few months later I received a call from Chris Poncon (owner of U.S. Fly) to advise that one of the U.S. Fly guides succeeded in fooling them with a fly that looks like a green salmon egg, as in the water it tends to stretch out and look like floating algae. This fly is fished by drifting it back to waiting milk fish that lie in the tidal current stream and suck in passing algae and other vegetation.

Russ Fisher, fishing buddy and BTU Research Committee Chair, labors to create a fly that might interest the powerful milk fish.

Fishing buddy, Mike Smith (left), and U.S. Fly guide proudly showing a successful milk fish catch.

Hooking them is only step one as it turns out they fight harder than a bonefish and put on an aerial show like a tarpon. Only about 20% of those hooked ever get landed.

How long this new diversion will last is anyone's guess. Will the milk fish move away from the pressure or will they just get wise. But, while it lasts, enjoy!

The Seychelles government has since made a change of the franchise holders for the fishing operations, giving the entire allotment of rods to Shackelton who have been very successful operators of the Ponoi River salmon camps in Russia and other fishing destinations, including Mangrove Cay in the Bahamas.

The Seychelles are truly an exciting and enjoyable fishing destination. Will it last? Why take a chance, suck it up and endure the long hours of travel and give it a try. The best time of the year is usually January through March.

The Florida Keys are a vast area and are known to most bonefishermen. I will not attempt to do a detailed area by area description of the Florida Keys fish as that would be a worthy subject for a book unto itself.

However, there are a few pieces of information worth passing along.

The Florida Keys Guides Association has over 200 members and a list of guides can be obtained at their website: floridakeysfishingguidesassociation.org. There are numerous outfitters who provide tackle and guide booking services up and down the length of the Keys. Sandy Moret's Florida Keys Outfitters in Islamorada, World Wide Sportsman (worth a stop just to see it), the Lorelei, Bud N Mary's, to name a few.

Bonefishing the Keys is not an easy game but it can be quite rewarding as the Florida Keys are home to some of the largest bonefish in the world and have been the fishery to produce several world records. Although by no means isolated to the middle and upper Keys fishing in this area tends to be both more productive and more easily accessible.

To access many of the camps mentioned in this chapter and other viable fishing destinations, I would suggest you make contact with Frontiers. I have used them for many years as my sporting booking agent and have had many wonderful trips. Located in Gibsonia, Pennsylvania, they can be accessed at (800) 245-1950 or via the Internet at www.frontierstrvl.com.

CHAPTER VII

Let's Go Fishing

There are probably as many opinions on how to catch bonefish as there are fishermen (or guides) and no doubt many of them have more than one opinion. The thoughts expressed here are a compilation of my own experience, the thoughtful input from my fellow fishing friends, the advice of many guides who suffered through my mistakes, and information I have received in various Bonefish & Tarpon Unlimited seminars and research reports. Elsewhere in this book we will highlight the more popular geographic locations to fish, and discuss some of the more effective techniques in each location, but the thoughts in this chapter are intended to be more generic and general in nature.

There are many techniques to fish for bonefish; live bait, artificial casting lures, and flies. My early memories and experiences with bonefish were primarily with jigs and live bait, and although effective and successful, once one is bitten by the fly fishing bug (no pun intended) one quickly assumes this is the only proper way to pursue such a worthy target.

One high probability way to catch bonefish is going to an area known to have fish, stake up the boat, toss out a bunch of crushed shrimp chum or a chum tube, hook a big shrimp on a spinning line, throw it out in the middle of the chum and sit back and wait. You might get even better results if you wait for a fish or small school to show themselves in the chum and then cast your shrimp to them. The only critical issue in this equation is how far to lead the fish to avoid spooking him. Lead is as intuitive as throwing a football but should also reflect the immediate conditions. That is, if the water is fairly deep, 18" plus, with a bit of chop on the top of the water and the sun is behind you, you may get by with putting the bait as close as 3 to 4 feet in front of the target.

It's a fine line between a perfectly judged lead that the target fish rushes to pick up and run with, and an almost identically placed cast that causes the fish to bolt like he had been banged on the tail with a sharp stick. Putting the bait or fly where you want it is understandably a matter of skill and experience but whether the fish jumps it or runs from it requires a fair bit of good fortune, or as they say in golf the rub of the green.

You can improve your odds by keeping the bait directly in front of the fish as much as possible. More times than not, if the fly or bait lands behind or to the side of the fish, it is more likely to spook him than if it is in front of him. There is some logic to this, as the fish is used to its quarry running away from it rather than coming towards it.

Hopefully by now the fish has picked up your bait and you have experienced that magic sound of line screaming off your reel creating the physical bond that will commit you to this pursuit for life.

As wonderful and rewarding as this scenario seems, I must tell you it pales in comparison to taking your first bonefish on fly. Having said that, if you are in the Florida Keys or other areas that experienced and pressured fish habitat in, it is not a bad idea to spend a few days fishing with bait to begin to understand the general ecology of the flats and the bonefish's movements relative to that environment.

Assuming one is fishing by boat, a good idea for the first day of fly fishing is to pick a likely scenario to produce fish and stake up the boat to create a little friendly shooting gallery for yourself.

An ideal scenario would be a flat where the tide is between mid-rise and mid-fall with a reasonable tidal flow, with the sun behind you and your target spot down wind and down tide of your position. The importance of this is three-fold.

1. The fish will normally work into the tide in their quest for food.
2. With the wind over your left shoulder gives the easiest cast to execute.

3. With the sun behind or above us to give us good vis-
    ibility and also having the sun in the fish's eyes to
    reduce the chance of him reacting to our violent arm
    movement and other attention getting gyrations.
4. With the target area being down tide we also create a
    scenario where tidal drift on our fly won't be a factor
    and where the tide will help straighten our leader giv-
    ing us a fly ready to respond to our strip/retrieve.

We can even further improve the odds of this scenario by chum-
ming up an area about 40 feet or for a comfortable cast, down wind,
down tide of the boat.

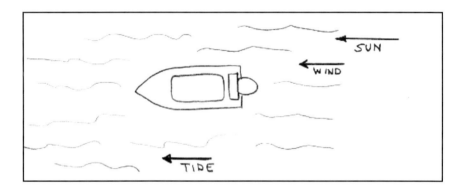

The perfect scenario—wind, sun and tide moving in
the same direction improves the odds of the hook up.

A fly fishing purist would be loath to use chum, but in your
early days of bonefishing my suggestion is to use every advantage
you can create to put fish on the end of your line.

To chum, the shrimp or blue crab are broken into pieces and
tossed to the desired area. I actually use a chum tube which is a 3"
diameter PVC pipe about 12" long with ¼ inch diameter holes all
along the pipe and threaded caps on each end. This works really
well, it is easy to throw to the desired location, it has enough
weight to stay put with enough buoyancy to have one end float off
the bottom to improve the flow-through water effect. We add a 10"

diameter hoop of plastic tubing through one of the end caps to make it easy to retrieve with the push pole foot.

An easy to build chum tube provides an added edge for the beginning angler.

As simple as it is, this little fisherman's friend will certainly increase your odds of seeing fish. As the scent feeds out through the water it attracts not only bones, but potential other desirables like permit.

It takes a little work to create this hypothetical ideal scenario but even if we only get a couple of the elements right, we have improved our odds of putting the fly in position for a hookup.

We are now ready to fish, so let's strip out about 15 double arm length pulls of fly line and then pull it length by length between our hands to stretch the cold memory curl out of the line. Next, we will attach a fly with slightly weighted eyes and a shrimpy look to it.

We will allow about 16 to 20 feet of line to extend beyond the rod end and carefully hold the fly between the index finder and thumb of our left hand so we know exactly where it is, and more importantly where it isn't. i.e. Not hooked on the boat rail, caught on a weed, etc. The weighted fly will help us be sure it gets down to the bottom in a reasonable amount of time before we start stripping.

OK, now make a few test casts to the target area so we are comfortable with exactly how the wind and tide, etc. will affect our cast and then start watching.

It is most likely the fish will come from down current but it's far from a given so we need to be diligent in our watchful waiting. Everyone has their own technique of looking and for sure some are a lot better at it than others and than I am, but I try to make a radar type scan of the sun illuminated visible area of the water, varying the scan from close in to one further out. It is quite surprising the amount of territory you can capture in a single gaze, once you have a bit of practice and success in seeing what you are looking for.

Since we are fishing in about 18" of water in our hypothetical scenario, I will focus my gaze and effort on the bottom, and in water columns and for water pushes, rather than looking for tails. I will look to try to see small puffs of mud from a feeding fish, the shadow or silhouette of a moving fish, or the surface disturbance of multiple fish under motion.

A good guide earns his keep in many ways, but two of those ways are picking a spot that is likely to have fish and another is being able to see them when they are there. We discuss some of their other many talents as we go on.

Hopefully you will be lucky enough to have some fish move into this angler's dream scenario we have established, make a reasonable cast, let the fly settle, and put a couple of good slow strips on the fly and hook up.

Unless you happen to be with a good guide in a fishery with an abundance of friendly (dumb) fish, you may not be quite that lucky. I am embarrassed to remember my first attempt. With a tailing fish at 50 feet down wind in front of me, my adrenalin flushed exuberance and desire to make no false cast and impress my guide, I was horrified to find the tail wind had dropped my weak back cast fly down and with my too fast forward cast, the fly made a perfect hook up on the seat of my pants.

My current guide / captain of several years and a beginning fly fisherman friend that often used to fish with him, use to vent their frustration by numbering their screw ups in their pursuit of his first hook up. i.e. 101—Hit the fish on the head with the fly; 102—perfect lead cast to the wrong end of the fish; etc. They made it to about 118 (starting at 101) before success was achieved.

However, with less frustration than I am suggesting with tongue in cheek, the major moment came when the sun, moon and stars aligned and a too dumb, too hungry, too aggressive fish knocked itself out to get at the fly, picked it up and took off. This success was regrettably met with a whole new set of challenges.

Challenge number one is to make a good strip set on the fish as he picked up the fly. Not so hard as to break the leader but sufficient to pull the hook tip well into the soft but tough flesh around the lip.

Next comes one of the most high risk parts of the success scenario, that is the part where just as you are half thrilled and half shocked that the fish has eaten, the fly line starts streaming out the end of the rod at lightning speed and the slack line between the reel and the first eyelet must be carefully fed into the eyelet without tangling, wrapping around the rod butt or reel handle, and without being caught under your foot. This is best accomplished by keeping both a cool head and a cool hand and allowing the line to slide through a loose tension applied by your left hand until the entire slack line has been fed through the eyelet.

With that behind you, take 20 deep breaths and enjoy the ride as the fly line continues to streak off of the reel, disappearing into the water in front of you with a typical 6 to 10 pound Keys fish. This process will take you well into your backing.

As the fish takes line, keep the rod tip high and clear of any obstacles. As the line begins to slow or stop and the end of this first run, keep your tip high but incline it away from the head of the fish to keep steady pressure on the hook and keep the fish's head bent toward the direction you want him to turn and begin your retrieve. One of three things will happen. The fish will allow you to begin to retrieve him, or it will take off again, or most risky, he may swim at high speed back toward the boat.

If it is allowing you to retrieve it, by all means do so until he decides to run again. If he takes off again, enjoy the ride. If he charges the boat you may need to take action fast. This could include a rapid reel retrieve but you simply may not be able to keep up, in which case you can revert to stripping the line in by hand, or as the last resort, simply take your rod tip down to the water causing all of the fly line to remain in contact with the water, and relying on the natural resistance of the water against the fly line to keep pressure on the hook, until you can regain control of the process.

The balance of the fight should be fairly uneventful but depending on the type of bottom can be very precarious and prone to break off on mangrove shoots or coral. If you leader catches or rubs on a mangrove shoot or coral, there is a high probability it will snap on contact. You can influence this situation somewhat by using a rod held high or by forced steering of the fish away from the danger. Regrettably there are times that it will simply be beyond your control. The fly line manufacturers love it because a fly line that may last years on a stone-free trout stream or spring creek may get chewed up and scraped up to the point of replacement after a few outings.

The most distinguishing and infectious trait of bonefish is its incredible endurance. A typical fish will make three to four runs with the probability of taking you well into the backing on each run and will still have enough steam left to make a couple of final short charges once it sees the boat.

As with most fish once it is tired you can elevate its head and bring it along side of the boat for the release. This can be done by an experienced hand without a net or aid. Whichever release technique is used, it is important to rest and revive the fish before setting it back on its own. Taking a firm grip on the area just in front of the tail fins allows one to move the fish forward and back forcing water through the gills to replenish its oxygen starved muscles. If fishing known predator infested waters one needs to take extra care with the release. If you have a live well on board it is even advisable to put the played out fish in the live well for 10 to 20 minutes and release the fish in a protected area such as along the edge of a mangrove structure.

As mentioned earlier, there are several advantages of using a professional guide, including forcing oneself to commit a specific amount of time to the pursuit. (i.e. One may give up after a few hours on your own if results are slow.)

However, if committed to fishing on your own there are several ways to do it. If you know the local area there are usually areas that can be reached from shore on some hard bottom areas that are usually wade-able. And of course, if you have access to a boat, there are always areas and flats that you can boat to and then wade with some success.

If you have your own flats skiff you can fish with a buddy and take turns poling the boat for each other. A more difficult pursuit but definitely doable is to be both the poler and the angler. Most that do this with success have developed a bit of apparatus to assist the efforts, such as:

- A rod holder to hold your rod and a fly line basket to hold the loose line until you are ready to put down the push pole and pick up the rod. I have a buddy who very successfully uses a milk crate for the latter purpose earning him the nickname Milkman by the upper Keys guides who see him.
- Able makes an excellent snap-in push pole holder that if mounted on your poling platform allows you to bend down, snap the push pole in the holder, pick up your fly rod and cast.

The push pole holder can be a real convenience and time saver for the self-guided angler.

● A stake out rope secured to the bottom of the poling platform to fasten to the push pole once it has been secured point first into the bottom surface of the flat.

Pre-positioned pole line permanently attached to the poling platform makes a quick stakeout a breeze.

There are of course those that use either a bow mounted or stern mounted electric motor. With the wireless remote controls available this becomes quite feasible, but still has some limitations on the depth of water required and a bit of a noise issue. To assist in surpassing the noise there are some stub-nose, 4-blade props on the market. This concept was originally designed by Doug Hannon.

Having said all of this, and even though I have some buddies who are quite successful as solo fishermen, I am always very pleased with myself when I am able to successfully catch fish from a moving skiff solo.

Essential to good fishing is obviously to find the fish, so see the chapter on fishing locations that are known for their abundance, as that is one good way to find the fish. The other is to either be lucky as heck or to try to think like the fish. Understanding their movements and behavior will narrow the odds of probable places to find them. (Also see the chapter on bonefish behavior.)

The following are my observations and some conclusions that I have come to over my years of fishing. However, I hasten to add that for every observed and concluded behavior there are an equal number of exceptions.

No doubt bonefish like most fish are motivated by their search for food and their fear for their own safety.

They will definitely feed and tail in very shallow water but generally speaking, they feel more vulnerable in these conditions and will spook at the slightest perceived threat. Having said that, in low light conditions of early dawn and late evening or even heavy overcast, they are much less spooky. I have seen situations in these conditions when you can hit them on the head with the fly and they will bolt a few feet and settle right back down. Because of their fear of predators aloft you will usually find the fish on the flats from mid-rise of the tide to mid-fall, and in my experience find these fish are less spooky and more apt to eat your fly than those you find at the end of the fall. It also follows that those on the flats on the early and mid-rise will tend to be a bit more aggressive feeders as they are hungrier.

Similarly in the late fall of the tide or early rise, the fish can sometimes be found in the very edges of the flats close to deep water channels where they feel they can beat a hasty retreat. In fact, you will often find fish schooled up in deep channels or pools at low tide where they await the next tidal cycle.

However, it is of interest to note that data from a study currently being conducted by the University of Miami Rosenstiel School of Marine and Atmospheric Science under the direction of Dr. Jerry Ault seems to suggest that bonefish may regularly move between the shallow water flats areas out to 20+ feet water depths of the inner reefs with some regularity.

This study is being conducted by implanting sonic beepers inside specific bonefish and tracking their movements with fixed acoustical listening stations located at various depths from the shore. No doubt we will hear and learn more as this is completed and fully analyzed.

In some cases when swimming predators are abundant the fish will abandon the flat at the higher tide conditions to avoid water conditions which make the movement of the larger predators easier and less detectable.

Dolphins (porpoise) are predators of bonefish. The dolphin uses his superior speed and intelligence to his advantage. If a dolphin senses the presence of bonefish, the dolphin will sometimes bang his tail on the water to make a loud sound to spook the bonefish and get them bolting in a single direction and then run them down. It's a jungle out there.

No doubt the presence or anticipated presence of food plays a large role in why fish frequent one flat versus another one and what day what food is prevalent on the flat. I wish I had a grasp and understanding of the food cycles to share with you as I believe this could be very useful. (See Chapter VIII, Bonefish Behavior & Biology.) Salinity or lack thereof and temperature play a big role in their choice of location as well.

Bonefish seem to prefer water temperatures in the 70's to low 80's, and dislike rapid temperature changes. Accordingly, a drop in water temperature below 70° will usually send them scurrying from the flats for deeper warmer more stable water conditions. However, if the cold conditions persist, they will sometimes return to the flats with high 60's temperatures rather than waiting for the 70° plus temperatures to return. On one occasion, to my own surprise, I fished to tailing bonefish in 61° water. (They must have been polar bear club members.)

In places like the Upper Keys where you have bay waters that tend to cool down faster than the larger ocean side waters, the fish will tend to disappear on the bay side first as the temperature drops and also will tend to move away from areas where the tidal creek connects to the ocean bringing the cooler bay waters into the ocean flats on the falling tide.

Another behavior pattern which can create some lively action is the one many in the Keys refer to as the ocean side push. Here you see several dozens of fish, moving in a large traveling school in herd fashion up the coast line, seemingly with a predetermined destination in mind. In the Upper Keys this seems to happen most often on the last of the falling tide, and more often than not moving north. I can't tell you how far they will go in a single movement, or why they mostly go north. Clearly they circle back or there would be one heck of a pile of fish at the northern end of the line. The moving schools are easy to spot several hundred yards away, as they create a very visible push of water as they move. If you position yourself in an area where there is a shallow obstruction or point which will force them to move around it, you can also predict their path with some accuracy. This gives you ample lead time to be ready to position you cast directly in front of the school. This is one occasion where a long cast can be particularly useful as it allows you to access the school for the maximum amount of time before they react to your presence.

My experience has shown me that if I can access the herd before or after the shallow area, where they have a more comfortable water depth, it improves the chance of a hook up. I have found that the lead fish are more likely to stop and feed than those in the middle or end of the pack. Similarly, accessing them from the side as they pass by is usually a waste of time.

I often fish this scenario with a medium size clousser. Having said this, if you happen to encounter them in a little deeper water you can often entice a traveling fish by fishing your fly up in the water rather than the usual bouncing along the bottom method.

When you catch the conditions right, additional schools will often be traveling the same route on about 10 to 15 minute intervals. (Where are they going??)

The presence of rays and small sharks on the flats are often a good sign that bonefish will be present, no doubt simply signifying the presence of food. Carefully checking out the rays is also a good idea as bonefish will often follow a feeding ray hoping to pick up a free lunch that is uncovered but overlooked by Mr. Ray. For some reason this seems to occur with greater regularity on some flats than with others. One flat that I like to get to in Biscayne Bay, you can almost make book that the rays on this flat will have a traveling companion. The additional beauty of this scenario is that you can put the fly right on the rays back, usually without spooking the fish, and with the knowledge that there is a reasonably good chance the fish will see it (and hopefully eat it).

Some of the behavior studies that the University of Miami has conducted with the support of Bonefish & Tarpon Unlimited (BTU) have shown that a fish will frequent the same flat on the same tidal cycle day after day. (See Chapter VIII—Bonefish Behavior) Although I believe this is truer of young fish than it is of full grown fish, there is no question the trend exists. Having said that, I have often had excellent fishing on a flat with a wonderful flow of fish on one day only to return to the flat an hour later the next day to find a virtual desert. (Go figure.)

One of the strangest phenomena I have ever observed was a period in the spring of 2003 in the Upper Keys. While the spring is normally an excellent period for bonefishing, on this particular year the bonefish literally disappeared from the Upper Keys for approximately 45 days. (Is this part of the spawning cycle?) Clearly the fish will school up and vacate the flats when they spawn, but usually only for a few days at a time.

Sometime on days after a clear moonlit night the fish may be hard to find or you find them and they just won't ear. One of the reasons for this is that they have probably been actively feeding on the moonlit flats where they can feed with greater safety and comfort.

It is a known fact that bonefish make clicking sounds. Do they communicate? One can't say with certainty but I have a strong suspicion they can. On more than one occasion I have experienced the following scenario. If I fish a closed mangrove bay area, with only one entrance and exit, there are several fish scattered all over different areas of the flat. After drifting this flat I elected to drift it again, but on the way in I pass a school of exiting fish. After this, when I proceed to explore the balance of the flat, all the fish had disappeared. One can only conclude that one of the fish gave the signal and the rest followed suit for a hasty exit.

This section would not be complete without a discussion of retrieving and hooking. Let's assume we have found the fish, and made the ideal cast in that magic spot close enough for the fish to see without being spooked. And let's assume we are in a position where we can strip the line in a direction away from the fish. The set up is ideal, so now it is time for the strip and hook up.

As I mentioned earlier, I prefer a somewhat weighted fly in most circumstances to increase the probability of the fly getting to the bottom in the area intended. If you can train your vision to be able to see your fly as most guides can, it will also improve your success at this most critical of all phases. Unless there are special circumstances, I prefer a slow 12 to 15" retrieve. This creates sufficient movement to attract the fish's attention and avoids sharp movement that might either spook the fish or pull the hook out of his mouth if he is trying to suck it in. It is usually most effective to let the fly pause for an instant or two before beginning the next strip.

This is often the movement the fish will make his move. The hook up is the most critical part of the game, but it is also the most natural. The fish will pick up the fly either mechanically with his mouth or most often by creating a water flow into the mouth and out the gills which draws the fly into its mouth. If you undertake a normal stripping motion when the fly is in the mouth, there is a good chance of completing the hook up. The hook up is obvious because as you continue to pull, the fish will do the same and the race is on. Conversely, if there is slack in the line when the fish picks up the fly it will quickly realize its mistake and spit the fly right back out. Opportunity lost. You can set the hook by lifting the rod but that is not as effective as the strip set or a combination of the two. About 90% of the time the fly will hook right in the gristle and rubbery tissue of the perfectly shaped lips. Unlike tarpon and some other species the hook ups on bonefish take very little pressure to penetrate and effect a secure and lasting penetration and attachment.

If you are fishing from a boat, one frequent cause of missed opportunities is underestimating or failing to allow for the effect of the boat moving toward the fish. As we discussed earlier, we are most often fishing down tide as the fish will tend to work up tide. Accordingly, when this is the scenario the boat will be moving toward the fish unless it is intentionally brought to a stop. In this circumstance, you may think you are moving the fly with your strip but you may simply be taking up slack created by the boat's forward movement. To overcome this, one needs to make longer, faster strips to effect the desired movement.

Another important factor when fishing from a boat is to keep the boat stable. That is, don't move around in the boat or shift your weight around while casting as these movements will cause the boat to rock and transmit signals to the fish that are very sensitive to water movement.

There is often a debate between fishing early versus fishing mid-day. I don't think there is any one right answer to this question. On hot days when the water is hot I generally prefer to fish the morning, before the sun warms the water up too much. Conversely, I fish later in the day on cool days when the water needs time for the sun to warm it. Also, I simply have a basic bias for mornings.

So set that hook, lift the rod, and enjoy the ride.

CHAPTER VIII

An Angler's Introduction to Bonefish Biology

Dr. Robert Humston

Compared to many other species of popular gamefish, bonefish have been studied very little by fisheries scientists. The earliest scientific publications focused on describing occurrences of the species and its unusual early life history. Some of the first descriptions of the biology of adult bonefish came from studies carried out around Puerto Rico by Erdman and Warmke; later Bruger would study bonefish in Florida waters, and Colton and Alevizon described bonefish in the Bahamas. In some cases, these early studies were hindered by the use of outdated techniques and limited sampling. In the mid 1990's Roy Crabtree and his colleagues published a series of papers which provide the definitive descriptions of the biology of bonefish from Florida waters, and recent efforts by the University of Miami's Bonefish Research Project have attempted to examine more aspects of the fishery for bonefish in Florida. From a scientific standpoint there are still many critical unanswered questions regarding the biology and dynamics of bonefish stocks. From an angler's standpoint, however, there is a wealth of information published that can help us understand bonefish behavior and better guide our efforts on the water.

Bonefish Basics

Bonefish belong to the familiar class of bony fishes called Osteichthyes, one of the most abundant and diverse classes of vertebrate animals. Within this class, ichthyologists further group bonefish within the "infradivision" Elopomorpha, which includes a few fish near and dear to the saltwater angler—bonefish, tarpon, and lady-fish—as well as several families of eels. Within Elopomorpha, bone-fish belong in the order Albuliformes which includes all species of bonefish as well as 2 families of deep-sea, eel-like fishes. The reasons for further grouping bonefish with these eel-like fish is based upon very specific similarities in body structure, but in truth adult bonefish do not even remotely resemble these close relatives. The reason that bonefish, tarpon, and ladyfishes are grouped with the eels in this way has to do with their early life history. In their larval stage, all of these fish take on an eel-like form termed a leptocephalus larvae: lepto from the Greek word meaning 'leaf', and cephalus meaning 'head.' These long, thin, ribbon-like larvae are nearly transparent and look nothing like the fish that will later raise your pulse rate on the flats. Their unique biology has been the subject of many scientific studies, and will be detailed more in a later section.

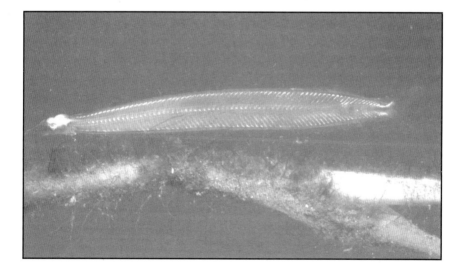

Figure 5: *A photograph of a bonefish (A. vulpes) in the leptocephalid larval phase. This body form is shared by the larvae of tarpon and ladyfish, and resembles their eel relatives in the Elopomorpha taxonomic division. Photo provided by Dr. Ivan Sazima, Associate Professor in the Department of Zoology and the Natural History Museum at the Universidade Estadual de Campinas, Brazil.*

The distinction of different bonefish species around the world has long been in question. Early on it was assumed that all bonefishes belonged to a single species; over the years as many as 23 different species distinctions have been suggested. Bonefish species generally are very similar in appearance, which makes it difficult to distinguish them. Recently Jeff Colborn, Ed Pfeiler, and a large group of colleagues took on the task of using molecular and biochemical evidence to tease apart the bonefish family tree. Their analysis suggests that the present day species of bonefish arose as long ago as 20 million years before present, and those species are identified as follows:

1. Albula vulpes, the most familiar species of bonefish, is the species which anglers most often pursue throughout the West Atlantic and Caribbean tropical waters (Figure 1). For long this was considered the only species in the Albula genus. However, the most recent molecular evidence suggests that there are at least 7 other Albula species—five of which have yet to be named and properly described.

Figure 1: A photo of a bonefish by Dr. Jerry Ault, University of Miami, Rosenstiel School of Marine and Atmospheric Science.

2. Albula glossodonta is distributed in the Indo-West Pacific, and is also known by the common name of roundjaw bonefish (Figure 2). Studies have identified this species as occurring from Hawaii to the Seychelles.

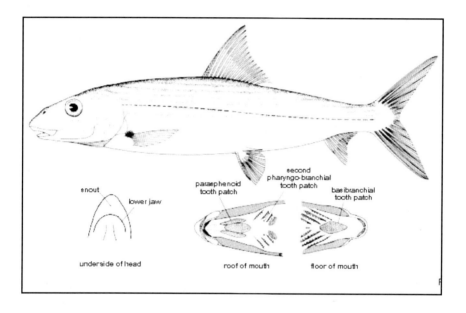

Figure 2: An illustration of Albula glossodonta, the roundjaw bonefish. Compare the shape of the lower jaw with that of A. neoguinaica in Figure 3, and you will understand why the common names distinguish them as the roundjaw and sharpjaw bonefish. Illustration from De Bruin et al. 1995, used with permission of the Food and Agriculture Organization of the United Nations (FAO)

3. Albula neoguinaica, also known as the sharpjaw bonefish, is found among the Hawaiian and South Pacific islands and all the way to the Northern Territory of Australia (Figure 3). This species has also been reported from the waters of Madagascar and the Seychelles islands.

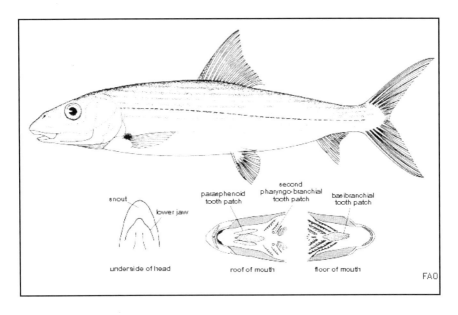

Figure 3: *The sharpjaw bonefish, Albula neoguinaica.*
Illustration from De Bruin et al. 1995, used with permission of
the Food and Agriculture Organization of the United Nations (FAO)

Figure 4: *Albula nemoptera, the threadfin or shafted bonefish.*
Not the extended fin rays at the back of the dorsal and anal fins,
indicated by arrows. Photograph by Jeppe Kolding,
Department of Fisheries and Marine Biology,
University of Bergen, Norway.

4. Albula nemoptera (also distinguished as Dixonina nemoptera), known commonly as the longfin, thread-fish, or shafted bonefish, is much less common and inhabits a smaller range (Figure 4). At present, it is assumed to occur in the West Atlantic and East Pacific from Mexico to Panama; some reports place it as far south as Brazil.

The exact ranges of these different species is not easy to pinpoint, given the difficulties of telling them apart. In some cases, species may have been misidentified and mistakenly reported in certain areas.

Body Structure and Function

Bonefish are unique in appearance, and are well adapted in shape and structure for their particular lifestyle. Their body is shaped something like a torpedo, streamlined for fast and efficient movement through the water. The extended, conical snout provides an effective front-end designed to reduce drag and establish a smooth flow of water over the rest of the body. The mid section of the body is stout and powerful, designed for rapid acceleration and sustained, high-speed swimming. And finally the tail of the bone-fish is tall (from bottom to top) and deeply forked, providing a powerful propeller to push the bonefish through the water at high rates of speed. Compare this with the longer body shape of a bar-racuda: the barracuda's body is designed for very short bursts of speed necessary for ambushing prey with lightning-fast strikes. When you see barracuda on the flats, they are often hovering at rest and reserving energy in a classic "sit-and-wait" ambush feeding strategy. Barracuda rely on their elongated body shape to help them catch prey off guard with their "sneaky fast" attacks. On the other hand, bonefish rely on their body form to help them swim quickly and efficiently for extended periods of time.

When a bonefish makes its first run across a quiet flat—and you can only watch as backing melts off your reel—it always seems like some sort of swimming speed record is being broken. It is very diffi-cult to measure the "top-end" swimming speed of fish under natural conditions. In some cases burst speed of hooked fish can be measured using coded fishing line, and other researchers have used swim tunnels to examine the sustained swimming speeds of different fish species. In his book Dick Brown lists some of the "burst" swimming speeds compiled by Beamish in his 1978 publication on fish swimming capacity; bonefish displayed a maximum speed of approximately 22 miles per hour. Wahoo were clocked at 37.4 mph, and sailfish at 67.1 mph. At first glance, this may make the bonefish's swimming abilities seem only average among sportfish. However, what these measurements do not account for is the size of the fish; by virtue of their size, larger fish generally swim faster than smaller fish of similar body structure. For this reason, it is often more useful to assess swimming speed of fish in terms of body lengths per second (bl/s). In this context, a bonefish clocked burst speeds of greater than 11 bl/s, wahoo about 18 bl/s, and yellowfin tuna at around 12 bl/s. At the other end, popular sportfish like Atlantic salmon only managed speeds of 6—8 bl/s. The reliability of these estimates is difficult to determine in many cases, but the evidence certainly suggests that bonefish rank high among contenders for 'fastest fish in the water' honors.

Bonefish are covered with overlapping rows of shiny scales which reflect the light and colors of the water around the fish. Like many other fish, bonefish are also counter-shaded: their color is darker on the top of their bodies and lighter on the bottom. This is a typical form of aquatic camouflage which helps them blend in to dark backgrounds when seen from above, and light backgrounds when seen from below. When combined with the reflective properties of the scales, these characteristics give bonefish the ability to effectively conceal themselves in remarkably featureless environments.

Moving toward the front of the fish, bonefish possess a very unique feature to protect their eyes. When viewed from above, it appears as a layer of transparent tissue which runs from just behind the snout and back nearly the end of the fish's head. This transparent tissue, called an adipose eyelid, protects the eyes of the bonefish and also provides further streamlining for the head of the fish. It is an anatomical feature seen in few species of fish, and it may prevent the vision of the bonefish from being injured or impaired due to debris in the water. This would allow them to forage in areas that contain a large amount of suspended sediments; for example, in sandy areas where they root for burrowing crabs, or in the mud trails left by feeding stingrays. On top of the bonefish's snout and forward of the eyes are two nostril openings through which the bonefish can detect scents in the water. Like many fish, bonefish utilize their olfactory organs and taste buds to detect the chemical signal of prey in the water. This is why live bait and fresh chum are often highly effective methods for attracting bonefish.

Inside the bonefish's mouth are first a row of very small teeth, followed by large, blunt "crushing" teeth which line the surface of the tongue as well as the roof of the mouth. These latter teeth are developed for breaking the strong shells of many different prey types, including crabs, shrimp and clams. The mouth itself is located on the underside of its snout in the low-slung manner typical of fish which feed upon bottom-dwelling prey. This does not necessarily indicate, however, that the bonefish only picks its meals off the bottom of the flat. Another popular sport fish, the redfish or red drum (Sciaenops ocellatus), has a similarly underslung jaw and is often taken on spoons, plugs, and topwater lures. There are many stories of bonefish surprising anglers by attacking lures high in the water column or even at the surface.

Putting this together, the characteristics of the bonefish's body shape should give you a good idea of its general behavior strategies. It is highly streamlined and capable of swimming at high speeds, which reflects that it spends much of its time actively swimming and seeking out food in preferred habitats. It can use both its keen eyesight and its sense of smell to zero in on areas that may be holding prey. The bonefish most commonly seeks out its prey on the bottom: when feeding the bonefish can use its mouth to either "suck" a large amount of sand / mud off the bottom, or alternatively it can also "blow" a jet of water out its mouth and direct it down into the bottom, displacing some of the substrate that may be hiding its prey. It then uses its well-protected eyes, nostrils, taste buds, and the tactile sensations picked up by receptors near its mouth and along its lateral line to locate prey around it. The bonefish can use its speed to chase down escaping prey, and prey with hard, protective shells can be broken down and consumed thanks to its specialized teeth rows. When trouble comes along, bonefish can use their superior speed to escape most predators that appear on the flats. As should be obvious, bonefish are elegantly evolved for survival in the shallows of the world's tropical waters.

1. Bonefish Life History

1.1—Spawning and Larval Development

There are many gaps in scientific knowledge of the life cycle of bonefish. The biology of adult bonefish has been researched to some extent; studies from Florida in the mid 1990's indicated that there is a clear spawning season for bonefish, which runs roughly from November to May. It is possible that individual bonefish can spawn more than once during this period. It is probable that bonefish in more tropical latitudes are capable of spawning year-round, as has been documented for tarpon and many other tropical fish species. However, the location of the preferred spawning grounds for bonefish is completely unknown. It is assumed that bonefish in Florida spawn offshore of the flats, perhaps beyond the deep reef tract that runs along south Florida and the Florida Keys. It is difficult to determine, as bonefish spawning activity has never been witnessed and documented. Many guides have reported seeing large groups of bonefish acting unusually around patch reefs during particularly cold weather periods, but the occurrence of these "pile ups" is neither common nor predictable. One hypothesis that has emerged from recent findings is that a specific spawning ground for Florida bonefish stocks may exist offshore of the Mid- to Lower Florida Keys, and that spawning activities are timed to coincide with the passage of winter cold fronts. This hypothesis is based upon results from larval fish collections, tag-recapture experiments, and interviews with veteran guides on the specifics of bonefish behavior patterns.

Larval and juvenile fish collections usually provide some indication of where adults spawn; as larvae are often at the mercy of current forces after hatching, their spawning origin can be traced back following typical current patterns. Unfortunately, collections of larval and juvenile bonefish have not provided definitive indication of where spawning occurs. Larvae have been collected in areas scattered around the tropical oceans including offshore of the Florida Keys, in shallow Louisiana estuaries, and in the Gulf of California. Unlike tarpon larvae and juveniles, they do not commonly occur within the bays and estuaries of south Florida but instead seem to be restricted to the eastern shallows along south Florida barrier islands. Crabtree et al (1996) collected juveniles and larvae from the shallow waters of grassy oceanside in the Florida Keys. In one unusual occurrence, juvenile bonefish were even found in the New York Bight near Long Island. These collections don't provide much insight into the whereabouts of spawning adults, which is a critical question in need of an answer.

As mentioned earlier, bonefish experience a unique early life history between hatching from eggs and entering adulthood. The development of their leptocephalus larvae (Figure 5) has been studied extensively to determine the mechanisms and function of this unusual larval development. It has been suggested that bonefish can remain in the larval stage for anywhere from two to six months, which is a very long period of time for a fish to stay in the larval stage. There is some question about what these larvae eat and how they ingest their food; some researchers believe leptocephalids are capable of absorbing nutrients from the surrounding water through the membrane of their skin. They have long, jagged teeth which extrude impressively from their mouths, yet it is doubtful that they use these teeth for capturing prey. Before taking on the juvenile bonefish form (which resembles a small adult bonefish), the larvae grow to approximately 65 mm in length. During the period when they transform into juveniles—termed the period of metamorphosis—the fish actually "shrinks" in length to about 35 mm. The adaptive advantage of this unusual life history strategy is still debated, and the answer may lie in the unusually long duration of the larval stage. However there is no denying its evolutionary success in species like bonefish, tarpon and their eel relatives.

1.2—Juvenile Stage

The juvenile phase of the bonefish life cycle represents another significant gap in scientific knowledge of the species' biology, especially with respect to Florida bonefish stocks. 'Juvenile' bonefish are young bonefish, past the larval stage but not yet sexually mature adults. In Florida, bonefish reach sexual maturity at an average age of 3-4 years and an approximate length of 17 inches fork length (the length of the fish from the tip of the nose to the 'fork' of the tail). Females appear to reach sexual maturity earlier and at smaller sizes than males. Despite extensive sampling of juvenile fish distributions in south Florida waters, small juvenile bonefish are only rarely found. Crabtree reported that most of the juvenile bonefish he was able to collect were found in shallow sand and seagrass flats on the ocean side flats in the lower Florida Keys. Juvenile bonefish have been collected in other areas with greater consistency — for example, in the Bahamas and the Gulf of California — however, these collections do not provide much insight into the habitat requirements of bonefish in south Florida. Juvenile bonefish are only rarely caught by anglers in any areas where bonefish are pursued, and therefore the specifics of juvenile development are generally of little interest to the angler. However, scientists hope to find out more about this critical life stage for the purposes of managing the resource.

1.3—Adult Phase

The biology of adult bonefish has been fairly well described in Florida waters thanks to a series of excellent studies initiated by Dr. Roy Crabtree in the 1990's. This research revisited results published by Bruger in 1974 using updated techniques and technology. Over 500 bonefish ranging from 21 mm (less than 1 inch) to 700 mm (approximately 27 inches) fork length were collected and studied to determine age, reproductive characteristics, and stomach contents. This comprehensive study provides the definitive data on Florida bonefish biology, and provides an excellent reference point for comparing past studies on bonefish from Florida and other areas.

By analyzing fish otoliths scientists can determine the ages of fish more accurately than when scales are used for aging fish. Otoliths are the essentially the fish's ear bones, and they grow in proportion to the fish's size. As the fish grows, annual growth is recorded in these bones much in the same way that growth is recorded in the rings of tree trunks. The otoliths are removed from the fish and cut into sections; under a microscope, the number of growth bands can be counted to determine the fish's age in years. Using this technique, Crabtree determined that bonefish can reach up to 18 years of age. This is in stark contrast to the earlier maximum age estimate of 12 years determined by Bruger using banding patterns in bonefish scales. Bonefish appear to grow very rapidly until they reach about 5 years of age and an average length of 531 mm (~ 21 inches) fork length, at which point growth rate slows considerably (Figure 6).

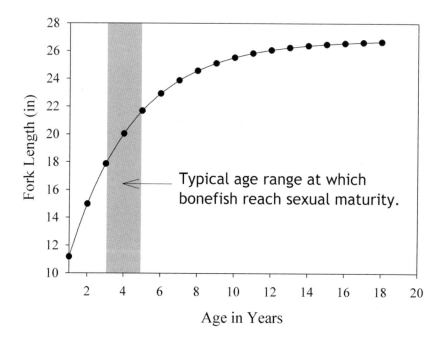

Figure 6: *Typical length (fork length, in inches) of bonefish at different ages in years. The shaded area indicates the age range (3-5 years) in which most bonefish reach sexual maturity; note how the bonefish's growth rate slows markedly after that age. Growth rate data published by Crabtree et al. 1994.*

Interestingly, this age coincides with the first years of sexual maturity (see above). This may indicate that the energetic costs of spawning are high for bonefish, which may support the hypothesis that bonefish spawn multiple times throughout the spawning season and that a significant migration is required to reach the spawning grounds (Crabtree et al 1997).

2. Feeding Habits and Prey Preferences:

Four studies have been published describing the prey preferences of bonefish from the waters of Florida, Puerto Rico, and the Bahamas. These studies analyzed the stomach contents of bonefish to determine what prey items are most often eaten. This technique is a standard method for examining the feeding habits of fishes, but it is not without bias. It is difficult to determine how the digestion rate of different materials can affect how often certain items remain in the stomachs of fish. For example: if the hard shells of crabs take a long time to digest, they will collect in the stomach contents of the predator fish longer than other items. They may then appear to be more prevalent than other food items when stomachs are analyzed. However, this method still remains one of the best ways to determine what type of foods certain fish prefer.

Of the four papers published on bonefish feeding habits, the most recent was published by Roy Crabtree and colleagues in 1998. Earlier papers were published in 1963 (Warmke and Erdman, Puerto Rico), 1973 (Bruger, Florida) and 1983 (Colton and Alevizon, Bahamas). They each differ slightly in what prey items they conclude are most important, but one common thread is clear throughout all the studies: bonefish eat a myriad of different prey. While they show a clear preference for certain species of others, the sheer number of different animals which appear in their stomachs indicate that they are — like many fish — generalized predators of opportunity.

2.1—Results from Florida Waters

Bruger published a single comprehensive paper describing the biology of bonefish in Florida waters, including information on age and growth, reproduction, and feeding habits. Since so much research was synthesized in this paper, it was not feasible to analyze the feeding habits of bonefish in great detail. Bruger ranked the importance of prey by the number of stomachs in which prey types were found, and did not report measurements of weight. The most dominant item eaten as reported by Bruger were crustaceans, mainly shrimp and crabs. Collectively, crustacean species were found in 73% of the bonefish stomachs sampled. Bruger identified as many families and species of crustaceans as possible and reported the frequency of their occurrence in stomachs. The most common items were Alpheid shrimp, a family of crustaceans known most commonly as snapping shrimp, which were found in more than 34% of the bonefish sampled. Xanthid (mud) crabs, Penaeid shrimp (e.g. pink shrimp), and portunid (simming) crabs made up the bulk of the other crustaceans found. He also found fish remains in 15% of the stomachs sampled, and mollusks (snails, clams, etc) in 28% of the bonefish. While he listed as many species and families of these animals as he could identify, he did not report how important these species were in the bonefish diet. In the end, Bruger identified over 60 different families or species of marine animals in the diet of bonefish from Florida waters.

When Crabtree and his colleagues later readdressed the question of bonefish prey items in Florida, their findings were somewhat different than those of Bruger. Their analysis was very comprehensive, and items were ranked not only by the frequency of their occurrence but also by the percentage of total weight of all items found (Figure 7). This latter measurement may provide more insight into how much certain prey items actually contribute to the nourishment needs of bonefish, as opposed to simply how often they are eaten. While crustaceans were still the dominant food type, he reported that fish species appeared to be more important in the diet of bonefish than was previously thought. Four families of crustaceans accounted for nearly 60% of the total stomach contents by weight; however, a single species of toadfish alone accounted for more than 17%. Collectively, remains of 17 different fish species were found in over 44% of the stomachs sampled and comprised more than 20% of the total stomach contents by weight. Gulf toadfish (Opsanus beta) were found in nearly 30% of the stomachs. This starkly contrasts with Bruger's lower estimation of the importance of fish in the bonefish diet. Furthermore, Bruger did not identify a single toadfish in the stomach contents of any of the bonefish he sampled. The reasons for this disparity are unclear, but it certainly suggests that fish—principally gulf toadfish—are eaten more often by bonefish than was once thought. Perhaps anglers should not be so surprised the next time a bonefish attacks their swimming plug!

However, perhaps it should not come as a surprise that toadfish are eaten as prey by bonefish. Toadfish are a soft-bodied, bottom-dwelling species that inhabits the same shallow sand and seagrass environments in which bonefish are commonly found. They have a highly camouflaged, mottled coloration that allows them to blend in with seagrass and benthic debris; they are even capable of burrowing in soft sand and muddy bottoms. Unlike bonefish, their predation strategy presumably does not involve much active swimming; they are more suited to "sit-and-wait" ambush tactics. They use their natural camouflage to hide from prey until it comes within reach of a quick lunge of their oversized mouths. When rooting for other bottom-dwelling prey, bonefish would undoubtedly encounter many toadfish in the same areas. Toadfish are not equipped for high performance swimming and do not have any sort of "body armor" in the form of prominent scales or fin spines, making them highly susceptible prey. Since they eat many of the same prey items as bonefish, they simply represent a middle-man in the food web. Bonefish would not be effective as predators if they did not take advantage of such prey types when the opportunity arises.

Crabtree's results also underscore the importance of several key species of crustaceans in the diet of Florida bonefish. Most notably, Xanthid crabs appear to be the most common item eaten by bonefish both in number and weight (50% and 30%, respectively). Species of the xanthid crabs family (of which the popular stone crab is a prominent member) are commonly known as mud crabs, and all share very similar appearances. They can be found in both soft and hard bottom areas, and are able to burrow in soft substrates. They are small crabs with hard shells and are generally slow moving and poor swimmers. This may make them more susceptible to predation by bonefish. Alpheid shrimp were the second most abundant crustacean family, particularly Alpheus floridanus. These are small shrimp with a single enlarged claw; they are able to "snap" this claw shut with such force that it produces an audible noise (hence their common name, snapping shrimp). They inhabit many of the same areas as Xanthid crabs and are also able to burrow in soft substrates. Bonefish could possibly key in on the noise these shrimp make as a way of locating and capturing them.

Portunid (swimming) crabs ranked third in importance among crustaceans in Crabtree et al.'s study. These include the familiar blue crab, as well as the myriad of crabs commonly seen clinging to flotsam washed off the flats with the tide. Blue crabs and pink shrimp (Penaeus duorarum) are undoubtedly the most common baits used in Florida to capture bonefish. However, their relative importance in the diet of bonefish sampled by Crabtree et al. suggests they are more common as bait than they are as prey items. Swimming crabs (primarily species of the Callinectes genus) collectively made up only 10.9 % of the total diet by weight, and Penaeid shrimp only 7.7%.

The study also compared differences among the diets of bonefish of various sizes and from different habitats. The most significant finding of this aspect of the study concerns the change in prey items with the size of bonefish. Crabtree et al. split their sample of bonefish into two groups—those larger than about 17.5 inches fork length, and those smaller than this size—and looked for differences in their stomach contents. They found that larger bonefish ate more Xanthid crabs, Portunid crabs, Alpheid shrimp and particularly more gulf toadfish than smaller bonefish. Conversely, smaller bonefish appeared to eat more Penaeid shrimp than their larger counterparts.

An interesting note among the results published by Crabtree et al. is the appearance of polychaete worms in stomach contents, primarily of the family Opheliidae. These small, soft-bodied, bottom-dwelling worms were found in 40% of all stomachs examined, but only comprised 1.4% of the diet by weight. It is possible that their importance was underestimated due to the fact that they may be digested more quickly than items such as crabs, shrimp, or fish with bony skeletons. However, this result further indicates the generalized nature of the bonefish diet. While it has been concluded that bonefish appear to prefer certain prey types over others—Crabtree et al. concluded this by comparing the contents of stomachs versus the abundance of prey species in bonefish habitats—it should still be noted that bonefish eat many, many different types of prey. In all,

Crabtree et al. identified 60 different families of prey types and even more species.

Finally, a study published in 1992 described bonefish as an important predator of juvenile spiny lobster in the Florida Keys. Crabtree and colleagues identified lobsters in stomach contents of Florida bonefish, but they only occurred in 0.5% of the bonefish sampled. Some anglers report that parts left over from a Florida lobster feast make effective chum for bonefish, and this may be supported by these scientific findings.

2.2—Results from the Bahamas

In the early 1980's Drs. Doug Colton and Bill Alevizon examined the stomach contents of bonefish collected from the area around East End, Grand Bahama. Like Crabtree and his research group, prey items were ranked according to both their frequency of occurrence as well as the percentage of total weight represented (Figure 8). However, unlike Crabtree et al. they found that the single most important prey items in the diet of bonefish were bivalves (e.g., clams and mussels). All together, bivalves represented 40% of the total stomach contents by weight and were found in 66% of the 365 bonefish sampled. The remainder of the diet consisted principally of crustaceans similar to those found in Florida bonefish (Xanthid and Portunid crabs, Alpheid and Pennaeid shrimp) as well as fish species (mainly toadfish and the goby Bathygobius soporator). However, their results indicated that in the Bahamas the swimming (Portunid) crabs appear more important in the bonefish diet than the mud (Xanthid) crabs. The primary species of swimming crab found was Callinectes ornatus, which was also found in bonefish from Florida waters. The Xanthid crabs identified were different from those described by Crabtree's group, however Crabtree et al. were unable to identify the majority of Xanthid crabs found and therefore it is difficult to compare this result. The main species of snapping (Alpheid) shrimp identified was Alpheus heterochelis, which did not appear as commonly in Florida bonefish. Colton and Alevizon also found slightly more mantis shrimp (Stomatopods) in the stomach contents than Crabtree et al. reported for Florida bonefish. Finally, toadfish did not comprise nearly as much of the stomach contents in Bahamas bonefish compared to what was found in Florida by Crabtree et al. (1998).

The difference in importance of bivalves in the diet of Bahamas versus Florida bonefish is difficult to analyze. As is mentioned in Crabtree et al.'s paper, it is possible that bonefish are able to crush the shells of bivalves and ingest the soft body within while expelling the hard parts. If so, it would be easy to underestimate the importance of clams and other bivalves in the bonefish diet as they would be digested quickly compared to harder-bodied items. However, the sheer numbers found by Colton and Alevizon compared to those reported by Crabtree et al. suggests that they are much more important as prey for bonefish in the Bahamas than in Florida. This may reflect an abundance of bivalves in the Bahamas, or a relative lack of other prey items compared to what is available in Florida.

Colton and Alevizon dedicated much of their analysis to comparing differences in the diet of bonefish among different habitats, seasons, and sizes of bonefish. They compared stomach contents of bonefish from sand versus seagrass habitats, bonefish collected in summer versus winter, and small versus large bonefish using size categories similar to Crabtree et al. One of the most notable differences was that bonefish of both size classes ate dramatically more bivalves during the summer months as opposed to winter months. Small bonefish appeared to compensate by decreasing the number of Portunid (swimming) crabs they ate during the summer months, while larger bonefish did not appear to display such a specific compensation.

An interesting conclusion reached by Colton and Alevizon focused on the difference in diets between sandy and seagrass habitats. They suggested that bonefish in seagrass habitats fed more selectively, and supported this claim with their observations of bonefish feeding in these areas. In seagrass flats, they found that bonefish tended to pick out individual items and even chase down specific fleeing individuals. Conversely, in sandy habitats they felt bonefish fed less discriminately and instead focused much of their time on simply digging up the sand and ingesting the prey items they unearthed. This once again indicates the dual nature of bonefish foraging; while they clearly have certain prey types they preferentially select over others, they are still highly generalized foragers that take advantage of the feeding opportunities that come their way.

2.3—Results from Puerto Rico

In 1963 Drs. Germaine Warmke and Donald Erdman studied the diet of bonefish from the waters of Puerto Rico. However, the focus of their study was on the different species of mollusks eaten by bonefish and did not expand the analysis to identify other species found in stomach contents. They reported that clams and snails made up over half of the bonefish's diet in Puerto Rico. In an earlier presentation, Erdman had reported that the remainder of the bonefish diet was comprised of crabs, shrimp, and other species. Erdman further indicated that several fish species occurred with some frequency among the "other species" category. Like Crabtree et al., he also noted that larger bonefish seemed to eat fish more often than smaller bonefish.

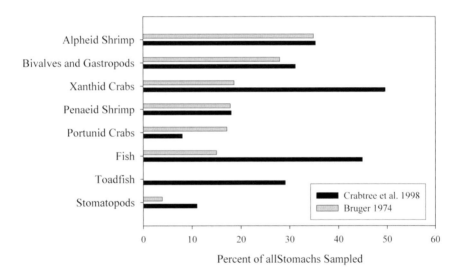

Figure 7: *Comparison of the results from two studies of the feeding habits of bonefish in Florida waters. Bars indicate the percent of all stomachs sampled that contained these major prey items. Crabtree et al.'s 1998 study concluded that fish and Xanthid crabs were much more common in the stomachs of bonefish than was observed in Bruger's 1974 study. In particular, although Bruger found fish remains in 15% of the stomachs he sampled he did not identify any toadfish (Opsanus beta) among these remains. Crabtree and colleagues found toadfish in nearly 30% of the bonefish stomachs, and mainly in larger bonefish (> 17.5 inches fork length).*

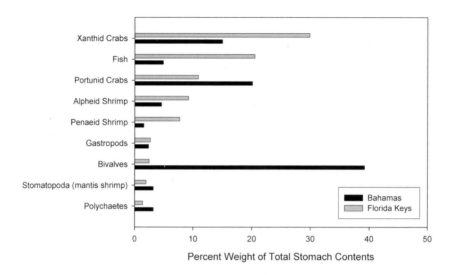

Figure 8: A comparison of stomach contents from bonefish collected in the Bahamas (Colton and Alevizon 1983) and the Florida Keys (Crabtree et al. 1998). Bars indicate the percent weight of total stomach contents comprised by each major prey type. Note that fish and Xanthid crabs (mud crabs) were much more dominant in the diet of Florida bonefish, while bivalves (i.e. clams and mussels) were more important in the diet of Bahamas bonefish.

3. Bonefish Behavior

Anglers are generally close observers of fish behavior, as understanding the behavior of the quarry is essential for consistent success when hunting the waters. For this reason, research on fish behavior—movement patterns, habitat selection, foraging, shoaling, etc.—is often of great interest to anglers, regardless of what type of fishing they most enjoy. Unfortunately, behavior is also one of the most difficult aspects of fish biology to study. Scientists have come up with many different techniques to observe fish behavior, with movement behavior and habitat selection among the most common areas of study. Conventional tag-recapture methods provide coarse detail on movement behavior, while advanced tracking and archival tags can be used to gain insight on fine-scale aspects of movement and habitat selection. These technologies have undergone decades of improvement and the latest equipment can be very effective, but monitoring the behavior of fish that inhabit large areas is still a challenging proposition. Research on bonefish movement and habitat selection has increased in recent years, with projects in Florida, the Bahamas, and in Pacific atolls like Palmyra. Much of this is due to the interest and support of conservation-minded organizations like Bonefish and Tarpon Unlimited.

Bonefish and Tarpon Unlimited (BTU) supported the start of a dedicated bonefish research program at the University of Miami, which has emerged to produce ground-breaking research on bonefish biology. When I was a graduate student at UM's Rosenstiel School of Marine and Atmospheric Sciences, I was given the opportunity to join a burgeoning research effort to assess south Florida's bonefish stock. The chance came when a group of concerned anglers realized that one of their favorite fish species was not being researched by any of Florida's fisheries scientists. I was a rabid-angler-turned-doctoral-student studying fish movement behavior, and when the opportunity came to study one of the most famous recreational fisheries in the world I jumped at it. The group of anglers was headed by Tom Davidson, and soon Tom, Jerry Ault (my graduate advisor), and I were planning the details of our first field efforts. The project continues to grow and expand its activities, which now include: conventional tag-recapture research, acoustic tracking research, and visual population surveys conducted by a volunteer fleet of professional guides. This coordinated effort has already produced some very interesting results, but it is only gaining momentum.

3.1—Long range movements

As mentioned above, the tried and true method of tagging and (hopefully) recapturing fish can provide some general information on fish movements. Specifically, they generally only provide two (sometimes more) known locations for a single fish. This information does not tell us where the fish was in the time between its initial release and subsequent recapture, but there are things than can sometimes be inferred from the time between captures and the distance between locations. For example, if the points are far apart and the time between locations is short, we can assume the fish spent the majority of its time 'in transit.' If more instances of such long-distance, short duration movements are observed within the same general areas or moving in similar directions, we might hypothesize that the fish are undertaking some form of directed migration.

Tag-recapture studies for bonefish have historically met with poor results, with very few fish recaptured relative to the number tagged. The tag-recapture program sponsored by BTU at University of Miami has distinguished itself as the first successful tag-recapture program for bonefish, with approximately 1800 fish tagged and 50 recaptured after tagging (Ault et al. 2002; visit www.bonefishresearch.com for more information). This recapture rate (2.8 %) is about average for tag-recapture studies, especially those which depend on anglers to voluntarily tag fish and report recaptures. Data from this study indicate that in most instances bonefish are recaptured within a few miles of where they were originally tagged and released. However, some amazing long-range movements have occurred which indicate that bonefish are capable of roaming vast distances within their regional range. Fish tagged near Miami in Biscayne Bay have been recaptured near Marathon Key and Islamorada, and fish tagged just north of Key West have been recaptured off Key Largo. These 75—100 mile movements represent fantastic distances within the bonefish's common Florida range between Miami and Key West (approximately 160 miles). Even more impressive is that one fish made the journey from Biscayne Bay to Marathon Key in just 15 days.

Attempts to track bonefish movements in the Bahamas in the early 1980's met with minimal success, and the conclusion that the scientists reached was that bonefish likely ranged very widely among the favorable habitats available to them. While the majority of tagging data may suggest otherwise, bonefish can and do travel long distances within the geographic boundaries of their populations. The reasons for these movements are the subject of present research; it has been suggested that long distance movements may be related to spawning behavior in some way. Whatever the reason, it is wrong to assume that bonefish are simply 'homebodies' which rarely venture beyond their favorite flats.

3.2—Home range and site fidelity

Conventional tagging studies have been helpful as a starting point for understanding bonefish movement behavior, but as illustrated above they have not helped researchers paint a complete picture of bonefish movement patterns. The fact that most bonefish were recaptured within several miles of their release location suggests that individual bonefish may inhabit a specific home range. An animal's home range is described as the area to which it normally confines its activity. Interviews with professional guides and surveys of anglers (Ault et al. 2002) indicate that many feel individual bonefish inhabit very specific areas or even individual flats. Such affinity for a very specific location is called site fidelity by fisheries researchers. Understanding whether or not bonefish have a defined home range or exhibit site fidelity is helpful for understanding how conserving coastal habitats can help protect bonefish populations.

To gather finer scale data on bonefish movements, a few different research projects have employed acoustic tagging and tracking equipment to follow individual bonefish as they go about their daily routine. In this type of research, fish are tagged with transmitters which emit a high frequency sound pulse. The sound is detected and followed from a boat using a directional hydrophone. In the shallows of the flats, a typical acoustic signal can not be detected from a great distance. To follow transmitter-tagged bonefish, researchers must stay close to the fish and try to keep up in the boat without making much sound. Any experienced bonefish angler realizes that this is a difficult feat to accomplish for any great length of time!

To aid this type of research, engineers have developed hydrophones which can be moored in the water and left to monitor the sound waves without requiring the presence of the researcher. By surrounding specific areas with these remote listening stations, University of Miami scientists have been able to gain specific insights into the possible home range and site fidelity of bonefish (Humston et al. in prep). Results from research in 2002 indicated that the majority of fish captured and released with transmitters on a specific flat were detected within that flat area for multiple days after release. Most fish returned for several days in a row, then left the area for good. However, other fish were detected in the area every day for periods of 40 to 61 days, after which it can be assumed the batteries in the transmitters expired. In at least one case, the data suggested that the individual bonefish never ventured outside of the approximately 1 km2 area being monitored. This particular fish was later recaptured by anglers fishing the same flat, almost 70 days after it had been originally released.

Previous studies in the Bahamas were only able to detect a few bonefish within the same area for up to 5 days immediately following release, after which the fish were never relocated. This led to the tentative conclusion that bonefish do not exhibit site fidelity and do not inhabit a specific home range, but instead they roam far and wide within their available habitats and remain in a specific area for less than a week. Some results from Florida are consistent with the Bahamas study, but others suggest that some bonefish may stay around a single flat for two months and perhaps longer. This may be a function of age, as the fish observed returning daily to the flat in Florida were smaller than the average bonefish caught by Florida anglers. Perhaps bonefish begin to range more widely after they reach sexual maturity, or after they attain a certain size. At that point they may behave more like transient residents of certain flats, spending a few days at a time in an area and then moving on. While the original research from Miami has indicated site fidelity is a definite issue, it has not adequately defined a home range for bonefish. Current research is increasing the number of monitoring stations and expanding the study area to address this question.

3.3—Fine-scale movement and habitat selection

The long-range and "meso-scale" movement behaviors described above are likely of interest to the angler only in a broad, general sense. For example, it is interesting to know that bonefish may vacate an area completely after being there for a few days in a row; but in terms of fishing, it only provides a new excuse we can offer for not finding fish where we expected them. The short-term, fine-scale movement behavior and habitat selection patterns of bonefish are probably of greater interest and utility for the bonefisher. These behaviors help us home in on the specific areas to look for bonefish when we think we're in the correct general vicinity.

In terms of habitat preferences, even the oldest scientific studies generally agree that bonefish can most often be found in shallow sand and seagrass flats along coastal shorelines and in lagoons and estuaries. They also move into deeper water in channels and out to the shallow reef line. It is assumed that they do most of their foraging on the flats, but given their opportunistic nature they are not very likely to pass up a meal whenever it is convenient. The interesting question is: how much time do they spend on the flats versus in the deep water, and what dictates this behavior? The earliest tracking studies of bonefish—which took place near East End of Grand Bahama—observed an interesting movement patter correlating preferred water depth with changes in tide stage. The fish they tracked would generally move into deep water on an ebbing tide, then back into shallow water as the tide rose again. This pattern was consistent during the day and at night. The telemetry research in Biscayne Bay revealed that Florida bonefish behave in a similar manner with respect to tide stage. In this study, bonefish were observed holding in a specific area of deeper water just off the shallow flat as the tide rose. When tide height reached its peak, the fish moved back on to the flat. This movement pattern is likely most prevalent in areas where the flats become extremely shallow at low tide, making them less accessible to the fish.

Conventional wisdom of Florida anglers and guides has long held that bonefish are sensitive to changes in water temperature. It is the experience of many that when water temperatures rise above or fall below critical levels on the flat, bonefish will not appear in good numbers. Researchers in the Bahamas did not note a movement pattern correlating with temperature in their tracking studies. However, they did notice that the number of "large" bonefish captured—which they defined as bonefish larger than 21" to the fork of the tail—declined quickly as water temperatures increased on the flats they sampled. They did not see the same decline in numbers of small bonefish, which led them to suggest that the avoidance of warm water may be related to the onset of sexual maturity and the development of sperm and eggs for reproduction. The observation of Bahamas anglers and divers was that these large bonefish would move into deeper waters (15-25 m) during these warm periods.

Based on the available data (Crabtree et al. 1994; Humston 2001; Ault et al. 2002), the majority of bonefish caught in Florida are past the age associated with the onset of sexual maturity (3—4 years old). If adult bonefish are likely to be sensitive to changes in water temperature, then Florida anglers would definitely notice such a behavioral pattern in the bonefish they most often encounter. Data collected in the University of Miami's telemetry study support the hypothesis that bonefish move into deeper water when temperature on the flats gets too high. In this study, fish were observed in the deep channels mostly during the warm summer months. Bonefish spent more time in deep channels when the air temperatures increased to their highest levels during the study period. The shallow water on the flats heats up much faster than deep water areas, and these deep channels probably represent a temporary refuge for bonefish until the flats become more hospitable. Again, observations by Florida guides and anglers generally support this idea.

3.4—Sound production

Bonefish anglers know that silence is golden on the flats; the energy of sound waves travels far and quickly in water, and an overly loud footfall on a flats skiff can spook a school of skittish bonefish in a heartbeat. It may come as a surprise to some anglers that fish can and do intentionally produce sounds, and many sounds serve as a means of communication between fish. Sounds made by various fish include simple clicks, booming "drums," and extensive "boatwhistle" signals. These sounds are often used in the context of spawning and mate attraction, but they can also serve other functions such as alarm or alert signals.

Studies have reported that bonefish produce sounds, though the mechanisms of sound production and its function have not been very closely researched. Sounds that have been recorded from captive bonefish ranged from 150—400 Hz frequency; these would be considered low-frequency sounds, given that the human audible range is approximately 20—20,000 Hz. Bonefish were observed emitting "toothy clicks, scratches and knocks" when feeding in competition with other bonefish. These sounds may simply be the incidental result of each fish's teeth knocking and rubbing together while feeding, or they may be sounds intentionally produced to communicate position and activity in the school. Bonefish could key in on sounds made by other feeding bonefish as a way of locating patches of food. Other studies recorded noises made by bonefish when alarmed or under mild stress, and found that they emitted more low-pitched "thumps and booms" under these conditions. Such sounds may be made by banging the gill covers against the body (similar to groupers), or by using muscles of the body wall to "drum" against the swim bladder (similar to members of the appropriately-named drum family). These loud sounds emitted when startled or under stress may function as alarm sounds. This might explain in part why bonefish are particularly sensitive to the low-pitch thumps and bumps made when feet fall hard on the deck of a boat. Whether bonefish may be attracted to "click and scratch" sounds like those made when feeding is the subject of future research by scientists and anglers.

4. Important Questions and New Research

Though bonefish are not subjected to the intense fishing pressure associated with high-profile, high-value fisheries—such as tunas or cod—there are still concerns about the future of this popular recreational fishery. Human development of both aquatic and terrestrial coastal landscapes presents unique problems that are the subject of many ongoing studies. At the core, managing a fishery requires baseline knowledge about the dynamics of the fish stock[1] and the impacts of fishing upon it. Predicting how the population may be affected by changes in the coastal ecosystem requires extensive knowledge about the ecology of the species; by definition, ecologists study the interaction between organisms and their environment. To manage the Florida bonefish stock through any future changes to the fishery or the coastal environment, scientists will need to gather and synthesize a wealth of knowledge on the dynamics of the fishery and the ecology of the species. From both perspectives, we've only just begun to assemble the biological picture necessary; however, recent efforts are making quick headway.

---

[1]. The stock is defined as the portion of the fish population that is exploited by the fishery.

4.1—Stock size

The question of stock size—just how many fish there are in the area being fished—is obviously of central importance when assessing and managing a fish stock. Unfortunately, it's also a very difficult question to answer with certainty. When managing fisheries, scientists usually rely on receiving data about how many fish are caught every year in order to monitor the relative size of the stock. It is assumed that the number of fish caught is, on balance, going to be proportional to the total number of fish out there. For commercial fisheries, these data are relatively easy to gather; for recreational fisheries, these data are much harder to come by. Getting a handle on the number of fish caught by recreational anglers requires either: 1) repeatedly intercepting anglers on the water or at the dock to count the number of fish they have kept that day (called a 'creel survey'); or 2) asking anglers to voluntarily give you an accurate report on the number of fish they catch, often by keeping a logbook of their fishing activity. Both methods require a great deal of time, personnel, and the voluntary cooperation of busy anglers.

A second option is to get on (or in) the water and count how many fish you see. This seemingly simple concept is actually quite a daunting task, and converting fish seen into the actual number of fish out there is not basic arithmetic. This approach has recently been taken on through the coordinated efforts of professional guides in Florida and University of Miami researchers, organized through Bonefish and Tarpon Unlimited. Over 40 boats took to the water on the same day with the goal of finding and counting bonefish, taking note of the number of fish they saw and the area in which they found them. As a result U.M. scientists were able to tentatively estimate the south Florida bonefish stock at just over 300,000 individuals in number (Ault et al., unpublished data). There is no way to consider this estimate relative to the number of bonefish in the stock in years past; however, the plan is to repeat this census every year to monitor the stock and watch for any trends or changes in the abundance of Florida bonefish.

4.2—Release mortality

In any catch-and-release fishery, there is always some question about how many fish actually survive the stress of capture and handling after they are released. Recently, Cooke and Phillip (publication in press) attempted to study the survival of bonefish following capture on hook and line. The study took place in the Bahamas, and the scientists used acoustic tracking tags to monitor the behavior and movement of bonefish after they were caught and released. They found that survival of individuals was high provided they were handled carefully and released in a "safe" location. Among other things, careful handling entails keeping the fish in the water as much as possible. During an extended struggle on hook-and-line, fish experience a build up of lactic acid in their muscle tissue—identical to the condition experienced by humans following extended exercise. Lactic acidosis (as this condition is called) is relieved by the influx of oxygen into the body, which only takes place when the bonefish is in the water. Therefore, anglers should avoid lifting a bonefish out of the water for long periods before releasing it.

The stress of capture also affects the bonefish's metabolic rates, which in turn affects their capacity for swimming. Though bonefish probably do not die of these combined effects, they can present other problems for a newly released bonefish. The reason has less to do with internal physiology than with the realities of the food chain. Bonefish are very vulnerable to predators following catch-and-release, during the period when their muscle tissue and metabolic rates are still recovering from the stress of capture. This was the main conclusion of the Cooke and Phillip research, as most bonefish that died in their study were killed by predators following release. Sharks may be attracted by the vibrations emanating from a line-hooked fish, and present a serious threat to any bonefish released in their vicinity. Sharks may not be able to easily catch a healthy bonefish, but a bonefish that is hindered by lactic acidosis is at a serious disadvantage in this contest. When sharks are in the area, it is wise to wait to release a bonefish or transport the fish to a safer area. A survey of professional guides in Florida (Ault et al. 2002) revealed that most were very aware of this consideration and were careful when handling and releasing bonefish after capture. If recreational anglers follow this example, the impact of catch-and-release fishing on the bonefish population can be kept to a minimum.

4.3—Habitat requirements

This area of research is still awaiting a great deal of exploration, and has the potential to provide very interesting and important information. While we have good general knowledge about the type of habitats frequented by adult bonefish, we do not have the same understanding of the needs of juvenile bonefish—especially the earliest juvenile and larval life stages. Fish are generally very vulnerable during this early life history phase, and require adequate amounts of food for growth and cover for protection from predators. It is important that scientists determine the essential habitat required for young-of-the-year bonefish, so that remaining areas can be conserved and protected for the future.

The recent tracking study in Florida gave credence to certain wisdom held by bonefish anglers and guides for years. In particular, it has long been suggested that bonefish are acutely sensitive to temperature and have a very specific comfort range. The behavior of bonefish tracked in Biscayne Bay suggests this may be true, but it does not give an indication of exactly what temperatures bonefish prefer. The effects of water temperature on bonefish metabolism would be useful to know from a physiological perspective, especially as it affects survival after catch-and-release. The exact impact temperature has on bonefish behavior is also of interest, given the looming threat of global climate change. There is evidence that bonefish spend more time in deep water during warmer weather; does this affect the amount of time they spend foraging per day, and subsequently their daily food intake? If so, how would a change in average temperature affect the behavior and growth of bonefish populations?

Bonefish are often found in lagoons and estuaries, where freshwater inflow can lower the average salinity of the water. They can probably tolerate a range of salinities, but there have been no studies examining the relationship between salinity and metabolism in bonefish. This is an important consideration in

Florida, where controlling the flow of freshwater into coastal ecosystems is a very important issue. Historical changes in freshwater flow have already had significant impacts on the inshore fish communities of south Florida. Might future changes affect the growth or distribution of bonefish in Florida waters? Understanding bonefish physiology and behavior with respect to salinity may help scientists answer these questions before any changes are made. This would allow scientists and anglers to give voice to concerns of bonefish stocks as future management of coastal ecosystems is decided.

The bonefish species grip the fascination of scientists and anglers alike. There is much to be learned from both perspectives, and new discoveries are equally rewarding. Just as the reflective surface of a calm, undisturbed flat holds promise for the approaching angler, scientists anticipate exciting times in the untapped future of bonefish research. As scientists and anglers continue to work together and learn from one another, the future conservation of this remarkable fishery is taking shape.

LITERATURE CITED

Ault., J.S., R. Humston, M.F. Larkin and J. Luo. 2002. Development of a bonefish conservation program in South Florida. Final report to National Fish and Wildlife Foundation on grant No. 20010078000-SC.

Beamish, F.W.H. 1978. Swimming capacity. Pages 101-187 in: Fish Physiology, Volume 7: Locomotion. W.S. Hoar and D.J. Randall (eds). Academic Press, New York.

Brown, D. 1993. Fly Fishing for Bonefish. Lyons and Burford, New York.

Bruger, G.E. 1974. Age, growth, food habits, and reproduction of bonefish, Albula vulpes, in south Florida waters. Florida Department of Natural Resources. Marine Research Laboratory. St. Petersburg, FL (USA).

Colborn, J., Bowen, B.W., Crabtree, R.E., Shaklee, J.B., and E. Pfeiler. 2001. The evolutionary enigma of bonefishes (Albula spp.): cryptic species and ancient separations in a globally distributed shorefish. Evolution 55:807-820.

Colton, D.E. and W.S. Alevizon. 1983. Movement patterns of bonefish, Albula vulpes, in Bahamian waters. Fishery Bulletin 81:148-154.

Colton, D.E. and Alevizon, W.S. 1983. Feeding ecology of bonefish in Bahamian waters. Trans. Am. Fish. Soc. 112:178-184.

Cooke, S.J. and D.P. Phillip. 2004. Behavior and mortality of caught-and-released bonefish (Albula spp.) in Bahamian waters with implications for a sustainable recreational fishery. Biological Conservation, in press.

Crabtree, R.E., C.W. Harnden, D. Snodgrass and C. Stevens. 1996. Age, growth and mortality of bonefish, Albula vulpes, from the waters of the Florida Keys. Fishery Bulletin 94:442-451.

Crabtree, R.E., D. Snodgrass and C.W. Harnden. 1997. Maturation and reproductive seasonality in bonefish, Albula vulpes, from the waters of the Florida Keys. Fishery Bulletin 95:456-465.

Crabtree, R.E., C. Stevens, D. Snodgrass and F.J. Stengard. 1998. Feeding habits of bonefish, Albula vulpes, from the waters of the Florida Keys. Fishery Bulletin 96:754-766.

De Bruin, G.H.P., B.C. Russell and A. Bogusch, 1995. FAO species identification field guide for fishery purposes. The marine fishery resources of Sri Lanka. Rome, FAO. 400 p.

Erdman, D.S. 1960. Notes on the biology of the bonefish and its sports fishery in Puerto Rico. Paper prepared for the 5th International Game Fish Conference, Miami Beach, Fla.

Humston, R. 2001. Development of movement models to assess the spatial dynamics of marine fish populations. Doctoral dissertation, University of Miami.

Humston, R., J.S. Ault, M.F. Larkin and J. Luo. Bonefish (Albula vulpes) movements and site fidelity in the northern Florida Keys determined by acoustic telemetry. Publication in preparation.

Pfeiler, E., Colborn, J., Douglas, M.R., and M.E. Douglas. 2002. Systematic status of bonefishes (Albula spp.) from the eastern Pacific Ocean inferred from analyses of allozymes an mitochondrial DNA.

Smith, K. and W. Herrnkind. 1992. Predation on juvenile spiny lobsters, Panulirus argus: influence of size and shelter. J. Exp. Mar. Biol. Ecol. 157:3-18.

Warmke, G.L. and Erdman, D.S. 1963. Records of marine mollusks eaten by bonefish in Puerto Rico waters. The Nautilus 76:115-120.

CHAPTER IX

Permit:
A Tough Challenge On The Flats

by Stu Apte

BIO:

Stu began fly fishing in the mid 1940s and began guiding anglers in the mid 1950s, in the lower Florida Keys, while laid off from Pan Am. Through the years, Stu has held more than 44 saltwater light tackle and fly rod World Records, including the two longest standing saltwater fly rod records. A 58 pound dolphin caught in 1964 and a 136 pound Pacific Sailfish caught 1965, both on 12 pound tippet.

The Stu Apte tarpon fly and Stu Apte Improved Blood Knot are standard items. The Stu Apte fly has also had the distinction of being featured on a United States postage stamp.

In 1971 Stu was inducted into the Fishing Hall of Fame. In 2003 Stu was the recipient of the prestigious Ted Williams Award and for the third-year in a row, was the Pro Celebrity Grand Champion of the Backbone Tournament.

As a natural extension of this passion for fly fishing he has written many articles for Outdoor Life, Field & Stream, and Sports Afield to name a few, as well as his book "Stu Apte's Fishing In The Florida Keys". He was also Angling Editor of Sea & Rudder, a national boating magazine.

In addition to writing, Stu appeared in ABC's Wide World of Sports, was field host on ABC's American Sportsman, CBS Sports Spectacular, Thrill-Maker Sports, ESPN's On The Fly, Walker Cay Chronicles , Sportsman's Adventures and the Teddy Award winning Sportsman's Journal with Andy Mill " THE LEGEND OF STU APTE", and ESPN's Out There. Most recently Stu is co-hosting The Outdoor World TV series.

The Florida flats from Key West to the Marquesas cover hundreds of square miles of shallow water over white sand. These flats offer highly specialized and vastly different kinds of salt water fishing for some species that, as a rule, are taken in few other places. One of the most challenging of these is the permit, a fish not widely known, but among the toughest to catch of all the wily prizes of the Keys flats.

For one thing, the permit is spooky. Warier even than the fabled bonefish, skittish as a brown trout, it is a finicky eater; a crafty, deep-bodied, hard fighting and stubborn fish. It's so difficult to catch that most anglers never even see one. Because of that, it presents the ultimate challenge of the flats and shallows from Miami's "Government Cut" to Key West, the Bahamas, Yucatan and Belize. It is a big, slab-sided fish with a sickle shaped tail which pokes out of the water as it feeds, tipping off its location, but barely indicating that just under the surface is a prized long-distance runner that may weigh 20, 30, 40, even 50 pounds.

Fishing the flats some many years ago with Bob Whitaker, a freelance writer and the outdoor editor of the Arizona Republic newspaper, I saw a very large permit moving along the shallows. I was able to check its progress as it busied itself over the sand bottom. With an ultra-light spinning outfit and 6 pound test line I cast my crab about six feet ahead of it, and hungry fish accelerated immediately to suck down its favorite food. I struck, and a second later the permit was rocketing the other way, where Hawk Channel offered the protection of 35 feet of water.

Leaving a v-wake, the fish zigzagging, barreled under the boat, dove to the channel and back onto the flat, and flashed again to the deep where it turned sideways, refusing to be brought up. I stood on the bow, holding as much pressure as I dared, the sharp bend in my rod emphasizing that my light spinning line was nearly breaking. Finally, after a grudging 21 minutes, the big permits circled to the top, where Bob quickly gaffed it. Weigh in, it went a whopping 47 pounds, only three pounds under the heaviest permit caught on rod and reel. Since 6 pound records were not kept until a year later, it became the ISFA [International Spin Fishing Association] 6 pound line class record.

Normally found in the same areas as bonefish, permit like to stay closer to the channels because they are much bigger fish, and need the safety of deeper water. When a permit is freshly hooked it zooms away in a drag-racing run exactly like a bonefish, but its greater bulk and power are soon apparent. The average bonefish weighs about six pounds, while a permit may average 15 to 25 pounds, and may rip a screaming 300 yards of line off your reel in its initial run.

Permit, like bonefish, have shell crushers in their jaws; I've heard they can administer as much as 3000 pounds of pressure per square inch, which they use for crushing shellfish. They eat crabs, conch, and several other arrow-shaped and spiral-type shellfish. I've seen them dip down to pick up a shell, chomp down on it, then eject the shell fragments.

The best bait for permit is a small live finney crab, about silver dollar size. The hook, a 2/0 or 3/0 Owner circle style, is inserted from underneath and just inside one of the points that stick out on either side of the crab's carapace. One reason I recommend using the Owner circle hook, is permit have a very tough mouth and rubbery lips.

The second choice bait is a large live shrimp; depending on the fishing conditions, I either slide the hook in from underneath, straight up, in front of the dark spot in its head, so the shrimp will keep active as I slowly retrieve it in front of the permit [if the hook penetrates the dark spot the shrimp will die.]. The other way, if the shrimp are not as big as I might like, is to twist the tail off and thread the shrimp onto the hook just as you would bone fishing.

Casting either bait, keep it low over the water, and stop line so it skips across the surface before settling down. The skittish permit will spook from a big splash, and sometimes from the shadow of a bait passing over. The skittering action apparently imitates a very small and scared crab trying to get away, and spells mealtime to a permit.

There are also many permit along the West Coast of Florida. They hang around the flats, stay in deep water around buoys, docks, and markers, feeding on crabs and shrimp on the outgoing tides.

The single best time for me to fish for permit on the flats is when their favorite food is most accessible; dead low water, just at the start of the incoming tide, the crabs are scuttling around, and the permit are ready to feed. Some flats near the channels are good on the outgoing tide as well, and a few flats will produce steadily even during the high incoming tide. As a rule, large permit rarely go up high on a flat when the tide is going out, unless there is a deep channel nearby which they may use for an escape route. But like all guidelines, these should remain flexible.

Wading in the shallow water, stalking, is the most interesting, ultimate challenge of flats fishing. Find the right place, with a firm, sandy bottom, at very low incoming tide when the fish are likely to come in. Get out of the boat and walk quietly and carefully to the area without disturbing what fish are there. Naturally, you are limited to how far you can cast in such conditions, and you cannot get to close or make a lot of racket. It can be tricky. If a big school of permit, 10 to 20, are feeding on the flat and you cast across to the one you want, your line can drop on another fish and the whole school will spook, leaving only a cloud of dust. And, when you hook a fish, you are limited to how fast and how far you can move to stay with it.

Fishing with Bob Beech below Key West one day just before noon, I found conditions looking perfect for permit. Using a plug-casting outfit with 12 pound line, I skidded my crab under the nose of a nice fish which was leading a trio of others along the sand. About 30 yards away, the fish gobbled up my crab and I set the hook. The fish sprang away on a marvelous run and I bumbled along trying to keep up. Splashing, running, stumbling in the knee-deep water, I was getting soaked from top to bottom, but hanging onto the big permit, which I estimated to be something over 25 pounds.

I began to put some real pressure on the fish and gradually led it around toward the boat, where Bob was shooting pictures of the whole episode. As it tired and hung in the water between me and the boat, I reached out and grabbed it by the tale to lift it up. It was a heavy fish, bigger than I had expected, and as my hand encircled its tail it got a sudden burst of new energy. It began threshing side to side, just about drowning both of us.

Hefting 30 pounds up with one hand is not all that easy when it's a well-muscled fish. Right after the picture, I released it to go back to its feeding pattern.

A more mature Stu releasing a handsome bonefish.

One of the many times as a young guide that Stu guided Ted Williams.

CHAPTER X

Lunch with the President

by Don Bowers

I have been fishing my whole life more or less, or at least as far back as I can remember and have been a guide since for close to 70 years.

My professional fishing days started at a unique private club in Michigan, "The Old Club". The main target is small-mouth bass and there are lots of them. A good day of fishing could often result in 6 bass per angler between 1.5 and 5.5 pounds, and I usually had 3 trips per day since the limit for each angler was six. That was where my summers and early fall days were spent, and my winter and spring days as a bonefish and tarpon guide at the Angler's Club in North Key Largo, Florida.

I first guided at Angler's Club in 1951. The Angler's Club is also a very special place. It first opened in the 1930's as a fishing camp and gathering post for wealthy Northeasterners who would bring their live-aboard yachts down for a few weeks of relaxation and fishing with the local guides. I say Northeasterners, but the Ford's were regular guests and I do remember Arthur Godfrey being one of the early regulars who once brought the Andrew Sisters down with him. But as I remember they did more boat riding and snorkeling than fishing on that trip.

However, the club certainly saw its share of rich and famous over the years, most of who enjoyed a good day on the water fishing. And the fishing was plenty good in those early days.

In those days the club (camp) was owned by Cliff Campbell. The camp was later converted to a club but one whose operations were underwritten by the Ford family.

Key Largo Angler's Club 1952

Jimmy Albury was a regular guide at the club in those early days and I had to prove myself worthy as he would usually get the first call. Later on Slim Pinder and Dick Friday came along but I had my own following by then. Prior to our arrival there were a couple of older guys by the name of John and Leon who lived in a stilt house over by Broad Creek and they were willing to guide if the angler would swing by and pick them up.

Our equipment was a lot different. I had a 16 ft. skiff made of plywood with a 10 horsepower Johnson engine as my first boat rig at the Angler's Club. I used then and still do now a 12 ft. wooden push pole and pole the boat from the bow. We didn't have platforms in those days so your pole didn't need to be so long so we used closet rods as push poles. And as there were lots more fish around, having the extra height to find the fish wasn't such a big deal.

One of Don's early skiffs.

One of the biggest problems in the early days was that we used direct drive casting reels and casting rods with braided line. Casting distance and accuracy with both were a big issue. So even though we didn't have to hunt long to find a fish, an 8 fish day was still a good days work.

One of the special treats for me was the years that I was privileged to be President Hoover's guide. He would come down to the Club for a couple of weeks at a time. He and his friends would typically alternate one day of fishing and one day of bridge. If the weather was really bad they might switch it around a bit.

There were several things special about fishing the President. First, he always fished in a suit and tie no matter how hot it might be, and second, he would have nothing to do with sandwiches that were prepared in advance. He has his own way of doing things. When he would get in the boat he would say, "Where are we going to fish, Hoover Point?" which was in the Arsnicker tip. I'd say, "Mr. Hoover, there is no water there at low tide." "Well, let's go anyway." I'd run up to the end of the flat and could see it was out of water, but I had to pole for a little ways. Suddenly, we weren't going anywhere. With this he'd say, "Don, I guess you're right." But we had to go and prove a point. His ex-FBI man (Mr. Richie) would fish with him often, as well as Miss Miller, his secretary (I guess).

We had other favorite spots we would fish—Broad Creek flats and Cutter Bank. Like many fishermen in those early days, the President always wanted to get his catch in the boat as soon as possible. Maybe so they could get on with catching another one; I don't really know. However, I do know the President would wrap his suit coat around the reel with his hand in his side coat pocket and screw the reel drag down extra tight. It often caused him to break off and lose his fish but he would never admit to this being the cause.

As I mentioned earlier, the President never cared for pre-made sandwiches and so he would have the cook's pack him a bag of fixings which would be in his satchel. At about noon (he always liked his food), the President would say, Don let's pick a spot for lunch. He would bring out his satchel and start preparing sandwiches for the two of us.

So when people ask me how I like my lunch, I always say I like it best when it's prepared by the President.

I also fished most of General Motors Chairmen and Presidents. Bob Burger, General Manager of Chevrolet; Ed Kennard, President of Cadillac; Pete Estes, President of General Motors; Roger Smith, Chairman of General Motors; and Jim Roach, Chairman of General Motors. I fished at the Old Club for 69 years as of today, and fished most of the Fisher Body people. I have never had to buy a car thanks to W. A. Fisher—I was captain of his boat and he kept me supplied.

I also fished the Ford family—Benson and Edie, Benson Jr. and Lynn.

When I first started fishing at the Angler's Club there were fish most everywhere if the wind was okay. We even caught lots of fish where the main clubhouse at Ocean Reef is now. There used to be a small area about 25 acres or so and when it became windy outside, we use to go in there and catch bonefish and get out of the rough weather. I fished a lot at Garden Cove even though it was a 12 to 14 mile trip in a 25 hp boat.

In the 1980's fishing dropped off. I think on account of a lot of the people who ran the coast line every day picking up "square grouper"—the fish along the shoreline were just scared.

I had some other famous politicians as clients as well. Hubert Humphrey and even President Eisenhower, but they didn't take it as serious as President Hoover did and they certainly didn't offer to make me lunch.

Last but not least, I fished Mr. George Berry Jr. for about 25 years or so. Mr. Berry is the owner of Pumpkin Key—a beautiful 25 acre island in Card Sound. My kids used to camp there 50 years ago. My dog, Missy, didn't like it; the coral was too hard on her feet. My boats are now called Missy.

Don Bowers and one of his regular anglers, George Berry (rear right).

I even had a man die in my boat in the 70's playing a large permit that we had been trying to catch for a few days. He had several heart attacks previously, but he wanted to go fishing. That's just what happened. I received several nice letters from his daughters saying that was the way their father wanted to go—with a fish on the line.

Even stranger, I fished a man at the Old Club for three years but I only saw him once. Just sent his chauffeur up every Wednesday for a cooler of fish to prove that he was there.

Back to George Berry, who loves to fish permit. On one of our best days we had 16 permit on during an Angler's Club tournament but only landed six. Still a pretty good days work. Believe it or not, we didn't win the tournament.

During the middle 50's, I went out with Tommy Gifford and helped him a few times (I hope) on his boat, Stormy Petrol. When Tommy was a young man he used to row in a dory to carry his marlin back to the dock. I've seen a picture of him with a 3-or 4-hundread pound fish—almost swamped the boat. He also liked to find the big amberjack by the whistle buoy. He actually talked to the fish and had them with their heads out of the water to get the blue runner.

I also fished a man for tarpon who would take a fifth along (for snake bite). When the fifth was gone, so were we.

I am 84 now and still fish whenever I can. Mostly with clients my own age who don't mind that we don't do it like we use to, but we still have lots of fun. North or south there is nothing in life better than fishing.

CHAPTER XI

Not Exactly Fishing
(Alligator Fishing)

by Capt. Bill Curtis

From the time I came to Miami and Biscayne Bay in the late 40's, the pursuit of bonefish has been a major part of my life and has created a very interesting life for me.

Over the next 55 years I met some wonderful and interesting people, and fished for about every kind of sport fish in the ocean; but I would have to say bonefish have probably been my first love. However, there are a lot of very interesting seconds.

In the early days I was both a photographer and fishing guide. I did on and off water photo work for various boat manufacturers and even became quite good friends with Ralph Evinrude. It was quite by accident when I was going a photo shoot for Evinrude at Ocean Reef on a beautiful May day in the early 50's that I noticed a large and steady flow of tarpon past a particular point on the ocean side of Old Rhode Key.

It has always been my belief that the tarpon that hang around Government Cut in Miami in the winter migrated a short distance south each spring as the winter shrimp flow slows and as the mullet pass by that area heading further south from their spring spawn. That southerly migration only lasts for about a month and then back north they go, heading for their summer home off the Carolina coast.

Over the next 50 years, I made many spring trips back to that point that is now called Curtis Point, a notoriety of which I am quite proud.

In those early days with a flat bottom plywood boat and 25 hp Evinrude Big Twin (the biggest engine available), it would take a bit over an hour to make the trip from Biscayne Bay down to Old Rhodes, and that was in good weather. If there was much chop you just couldn't travel in those flat bottom boats at all.

Fortunately, most days I wouldn't have to go more than a mile from where I put in as bonefish in Biscayne Bay were plentiful. On a reasonable day you could almost always see your next school if you didn't happen to hook up with the one in front of you. Once spring came along we could often catch over 20 fish on a good day.

Those were the good old days of bonefishing. In fact, I would guess we have less than 10% of the fish population today that we had in 1950. Word of good fishing quickly spread and I had a chance to fish some of the real greats like Joe Brooks, Ralph Evinrude, Bob Hewes, Lee Wulff, Ted Williams, Curt Gowdy and many others.

As several of these anglers were accomplished fly fishermen, I learned to pole the boat standing by the stern standing on top of my Evinrude engine. This eventually led to corroboration between Bob Hewes and me to invent the first poling platform.

My favorite fly in those days was the Frankie Belle named after Frankie Albright and her regular fishing partner, Belle Mathers. I haven't used it recently but I would guess it would probably work just as well today as it did then.

My acquaintance with Bob Hewes also resulted in my working with him to develop and perfect the original 16 ½ ft. Hewes Bonefisher. The Hewes boats were the first serious attempt to design a boat specifically for bonefish and what a difference it made.

Over the years I have tried a lot of different kinds of fishing. Marlin fishing on fly with Joe Brooks, and taking a 44 Enterprise to the Bahamas which we used as a mother ship from which we would do skiff fishing trips for a variety of prey including a green turtle hunt. But probably my most unusual fishing trip was one right in my backyard.

Well, it wasn't really fishing for fish; it was fly fishing for alligators. It was in the mid-1990's when the Everglades was experiencing a significant drought. So much so that the general water table and water level had receded, and what a few years before had been covered with water was then a partially dry, partially wet area with finger tributary water flow. As a result, what game survived had aggregated around these tributaries.

It was at that time that a couple of dry fly fishermen from Wyoming came to South Florida with an idea to fly fish for alligators. How's that for something different?

We talked about it for some time and agreed to give it a try. The drought really worked in our favor by concentrating the alligators for us. We probably saw over 200 gators in the course of the day.

As to the dry fly gator fishing, it worked. We would spot a small gator and quietly slide the boat within casting range. These guys were expert trout fishermen so all they had to do was to get the large spun deer hair flies two or three feet in front of the gators. The gators were so hungry that they would go for anything moving on the surface of the water. After thrashing around a little, they would pull them alongside and I would use a de-hooker on a three foot rod to release the barb-less hook. The gators fought like they were on valium.

Well, it will never replace bonefishing for me but I must admit it was a very interesting day.

CHAPTER XII

Saltwater Grand Slam

by J.M. Chico Fernandez

I came to this country in the late 50s when communism took over Cuba. And since I was already fly fishing in Cuba, it took me only a week to start meeting the few fly fishers in the Miami area. Captain Bill Curtis, Norman Duncan (who invented the Duncan Loop), John Emery and Flip Pallot were some of my first fly fishing buddies.

My first grand slam took place, as well as I can remember, around the mid 60s. And my poling partner that day was the late Captain John Emery, a great innovator of fly fishing tackle, a college mate, a gentleman and a friend of many years.

This was to be a most memorable day for taking fish, for adventure, for reassigning lunch, for getting in trouble, ... you'll see what I mean.

I remember the day well. I have thought about it, on and off, for many years. And have told the story at several parties and fishing clubs.

It was early summer and the beginning of school vacation. The day was one of those calm steamy days, with temperatures in the 90s and water temperature close to it.

John had borrowed a small flats skiff with a 35 hp tiller handle and no poling platform, of course. The push pole, which had no designated place in the skiff, bounced with every wave. (I don't think many skiffs had push pole holders in those days; certainly not our loaner.) The pole was one of the old twelve foot wooden dowels so often used those days. And to prevent the user from getting too many splinters in his hands during a day's fishing, it had been painted white, which was a common practice. We felt the pole was light those days, but it probably would have tipped the scale at triple the weight of a modern push pole today. Still we where happy to have it. The wide foot on the pole was generally glued and screed on.

With a dead low tide, we left Key Biscayne, in Miami, and ran on the outside of the flats to avoid running aground. Even on a flat calm day, I remember the old flat bottom skiff still pounding, the whole 30 minutes ride.

Finally, after passing Soldier Key, with its tall Australian pines, John cut the engine off and we glided slowly until we touch the edge of the ocean flat we intended to fish.

Water was slowly pouring over the flat during the first stages of the incoming tide. At the Northwest edge of the flat, you could still see the remains of an old barge, mostly out of water at this stage of the tide. The sides were gone, but the beams would stick out pointing toward the sky. Often cormorants sat on the ends of the beams and hunt for small baitfish that made this shallow wreck their home and refuge. The barge had been there for as long as anyone remembers, and for more than 30 years it was a familiar sight for all of us who fished the area. Finally, on August 24, 1992, Hurricane Andrew dragged it into deep water and out of sight. We all miss it.

I remember that the flat was still too shallow to pole, so both John and I left the skiff and waded with our fly rods. But this turn out to be a very frustrating morning. With the extra shallow water, the bonefish that came to feed that day had their backs, tails and dorsal fins out of water. To say they were extremely spooky would have been an understatement.

If we crouched in our approach, we usually could get within casting distance, but any movement of the hand and rod, and I mean any movement, and they would spook a couple of hundred feet or so, and then start feeding again. They even seem to spook from our back cast, ... well, maybe I'm exaggerating a little, but you know what I mean.

We tried getting on our knees and waiting until they came within casting range, but it did not work. We tried longer leaders, maybe 15 feet long, but it did not work. We tried smaller hooks, (in those days a small hook was a #2, and a #1 was standard bonefish fly sizes) but that did not work either.

As the tide got higher, the bones continued to roam the flats but without showing their dorsal or tail, and against the dark bottom, we could not see them until they were too close. So we spooked them just as well.

An hour or so later, the bones were gone, leaving a pair of frustrated fly fishermen. We had run out of tricks. If they came back right then, we would not have known what else to try.

On the walk back to the skiff, John mentioned that the fish would be back 12 hours or so from now, as that is when the tide would again be low incoming. It would be late that evening, and we could take another crack at them. I remember telling him I never wanted to see those bonefish again.

TARPON TIME

Since it was still early and calm, we headed way down South around the area of Old Rhodes Key. This area had hundreds of tarpon in those days, and it was nothing to get a couple of dozen shots at them in a morning. This area today still has a few tarpon in the spring and lots of fly fishermen after them.

The only rods we had brought with us were a pair of nine weight glass rods. Mine I remember, with my Seamaster double handle reel. John had his Hardy Zenith in his.

I think we jumped a few fish that morning as we took turns, but did not land any. Finally, I hooked one and it stayed on, he was probably well under hundred. However, the fish only made a couple of "conservative" jumps and then settle for a long fight. All the pressure I could put on the soft nine weight rod did not seem to impress him.

He towed us in to the bay side and we followed a long ways behind. But then he reached a small key and for some reason made a complete U turn around the key, and headed back to sea.

By the time we reached the key, and were able to get around it and back toward the ocean, my leader, fly line and part of my backing had been scrapped against the mangroves roots. Now the fish was more than 150 yards away, and not knowing if the tippet was frayed, I was not too sure just how much pressure I could put on my outfit.

With the engine running we finally caught up with him in about twenty feet of water. It was then I noticed that my fly line was scrapped to the core in some areas, ruined. Please remember that the price of a fly line in those days was equivalent to a movie date, and dinner date! Still, I had the tarpon on.

Now in deep water, and against the soft glass rod, it must have been more than two hours before I brought the fish to the side. I still remember John taking the leader, and in his usual cool calm mode, removing the 4/0 fly from his jaws. I was in high spirit, very tired and probably now floating in more than 30 feet of water. Actually, we were lucky that one of the many hammerhead sharks that often patrol the area looking mainly for tarpon, did not discover our fish during the long fight.

JOHN'S LAST LUNCH ASSIGNMENT

Yes, I also remember lunch that day very well. You see, I have always been an advocate of a civilized lunch for a fly fisherman, even in those days—large Cuban sandwiches or subs, sodas and juices, potato chips, chocolate chip cookies, ... the bare essentials. And the tarpon victory called for a celebration. But John, who was always more casual than I in these important matters, produced a small cooler with two apples, a wedge of cheese and lukewarm ice tea. We fished together many times again over the next twenty plus years, but this was the last time I left him in charged of lunch. You understand.

WINDY? GO PERMIT FISHING

In those days, fly fishing for permit was almost an illusion. You cast to fish after fish with no hits. And if you got a boil, a flash or a follow, well, you had bagging rights!

The reason for today's success in fly fishing for permit, (many anglers have taken more than one permit on fly in a day, and some up to seven in a day) is partly technical. We know better how to work the fly. But mostly it's the flies we have today. In those days we did not have the epoxy flies or the crab flies that are so productive in the flats today. Our best fly, at least to my experience, was something called the Optic fly. A white marabou streamer with a heavy brass bead head, painted with a large eye and usually tied on a 1/0 hook, short shank. It would plop and dive to the bottom like no other fly we had, with the marabou seductively waving as it went. A few permit and some mutton snapper were taken in the 60s with this fly. It was precisely this fly that I had tied on.

After lunch, the wind had picked up considerably and we decided to fish for permit around a natural coral formation well known around Miami anglers called The Rock Pile.

When we arrived at the area, we cut the engine off a few hundred feet away and made the quiet approach by push pole, as it should be. Part of the rock formation stuck out of the water so it made it easy to see where we were going. As we reached with in 100 feet or so, a school of permit was milling around the deeper ocean side of the Rock Pile.

If I recall correctly, either the school started to leave the rock pile a bit earlier than we anticipated, or we approached the school from the wrong side. In any event, the situation required a long cast. Actually, it was a very difficult cast even down wind because I had a fly line with long slices of coating taken away by mangroves trees that morning. Let's just say, it did not shoot very well.

I don't think my cast quite reached the lead fish as I had hoped, but what I do remember distinctly is that two fish parted from that school and followed the weighted marabou fly as eager as a pair of jacks, and they came almost up to the boat. And then, in a spirit of competition I guess, the smallest one took the fly and before I knew it, the remaining fly line had cleared from my hands and he was on the reel. We were both surprised. We didn't "really" expect a hook up.

As the Rock Pile is right at the edge of deeper water facing the ocean, the permit headed that way, through an area covered with sea fans, protrusions of small live coral, sponges, and many other line cutting devices. I remember John helping me untangle my fly line from sponges and sea fans in four of five feet of water with the broad side of the push pole. But eventually as the permit got into deeper and deeper water, the obstructions on the bottom were no longer a problem and then it was just a matter of time before he came up.

Eventually we had the permit by the boat, and John lifted the fish by the wrist of the tail. We yelled and screamed at the sky, and then we put him back. I think we estimated him about 15 pounds.

I don't remember what else we did the rest of the afternoon, or if we caught any other fish, but I know that late that evening, with the sun close to the horizon we were heading home along the same ocean side route, because most of the flats were out of water again.

Before I realized it, John pulled up to the same flat we had fish that morning, cut the engine and then poled slowly to the edge. The barge was once again out of the water, and conditions looked the same as that morning. Except that the sun, now close to the horizon, shed little light on the flat at this low angle.

Soon we started to see bonefish again, this time their fins were dark in the low light, and I remember not being too excited, expecting the same problems as this morning.

This time the fish were not as spooky as they had been in the morning, probably because of the low light level, but visibility was poor, and we found ourselves casting to dark tails and often spooking fish when we lined them.

I remember having the worst of times, aggravated by the fact that I was fishing with a fly line that had lost several feet of coating that morning, and now often sank to the bottom and snagged, spooking bonefish just as efficiently as I had done that morning.

In the meantime, John took a large bonefish and I believe had others on. I continued to clear the flat of any bonefish with in casting range.

John, typical of his behavior, just approached me, took the outfit off my hands and handed me his. I don't remember any words being exchanged.

I managed to spook fish just as well with John's outfit, and as we lost most of the light I was ready to give up. Now the only recollection I have at this moment is that I cast to several bonefish tailing close together, that I thought I was snagged on the bottom again and that when I lifted the rod, (I don't remember that we "strip struck" in those days) I actually had a fish on.

I do remember the sweet sound of the Hardy's clicker reel. Yes, I remember that well. Actually, I still use some clicker reel today in salt water, and they are still fun.

By the time I landed him, it was almost pitch-black. And by the time we ran back to the marina, cleaned, returned the skiff and arrived home, it was close to midnight. I probably had left home around 4 a.m. that morning.

My parents were waiting for me in pajamas, (I seldom thought of calling and letting them know I was still alive) and they weren't waiting to ask how the fishing had been. As a matter of fact it was days before I could share with my dad, who was an angler, what a great day we had, that day of the court-martial. I later found that John faced similar charges at his home.

In those days, I do not remember such things as a grand slam. I don't think the concept existed. But I do remember a few years later, during a fishing trip in the Florida Keys with John, someone telling us they had just taken a Grand Slam. And John immediately reminded me of the now famous court-martial day.

Ah yes—I said proudly—I too have taken a Grand Slam. The court-martial charges did not come up, even though I was convicted and sentenced to many days of yard work and garage cleaning. Those were the days.

CHAPTER XIII

Doesn't That Beat All

by Sandy Moret

The mention of Deep Water Cay on Grand Bahama always brings a smile to my face.

This pristine realm offers miles of flats with lush turtle grass. Rummer Creek, Big Harbor Creek and the many other tidal sloughs have channels with current flow that are protected on the windiest of days. Even better are the acres of sand flats that provide firm wading on lower tide phases. Plenty of two to six pound "user friendly" bonefish make it a great angling destination.

The lodge provides great creature comforts, excellent food and a super nice staff. Three squares a day and a couple of Kalik's always cause me to let the belt out a notch or two when I board the plane to come home. The guides are really good fishermen, helpful and friendly. Each year they get even better.

Deep Water's people, beautiful setting and great fishing as well as its close proximity to my home in the Florida Keys, cause it to be one of my favorite places to get away for a relaxing long week-end with friends. My first trip to Deep Water was in 1989 and I have spent a few days there every year since.

I find on most fishing trips the "rule of one third prevails" and my expectations are tuned for it. One third of the trips I take are fantastic. The weather and tides are perfect. The fish are hungry and bite most any fly and the logistics hum like a Tibor fly reel. One third of my trips are average to good with a minor glitch somewhere along the way. Some overcast may make visibility tougher or the fish are a little harder to feed. It's okay, not great but not to bad either.

Then one third are not so great to poor. An unseasonable cold front may bring unfishable pounding rain, lightning and 30 knot winds. A paddle fan could grab a flyrod tip or even worse was when we ran out of cerveza in Mexico for a day! All in all like any seasoned traveling angler, you adjust and go with the flow.

A few years ago, my wife Sue and I were hosting one of our trips to Deep Water Cay for our fly fishing school alumni. It started out as a maximum best on the one third scale. The flight over was smooth and the weather in February was like May. We had a really special group of friends with high camaraderie. The trip turned out to be a banner experience with tons of good fishing, except for one morning I will never forget.

The morning was flat calm with that perfect humidity where the musk of mangroves at low tide fills the air. We could feel that the bonefishing would be bonkers on that day. Sue and I finished breakfast and strolled over to the dock with our gear. We carried our rods, wading booties, fanny packs and great attitudes. We were a little surprised when our guide from the day before was not to be seen. But it was no problem; Audley would take us bonefishing. Audley had worked at Deep Water forever doing maintenance, handling luggage, cleaning catch of the day and opening conch shells. We knew him from our many prior trips and always joked over his island stories that he related with his soft rich Bahamian accent. Having lived all of his life in Mac Leans Town, he knew the waters, tides and bonefish as well or better than anyone. It was just his first experience at guiding fly fishermen.

After loading the boat, we left the dock about ten minutes behind the other boats, which were almost out of sight on the horizon. We ran for about ten minutes and then cut through a channel that opened into a huge basin with scattered mangroves, firm bottom and a small channel that meandered for a mile. Audley shut down the engine as we entered the basin and as we glided to a stop there were acres and acres of tailing bonefish. I mean hundreds and hundreds of bonefish tailing and pushing as far as we could see. The tide was beginning to flood and we just knew that they would continue to feed hard for the next three hours.

I had a seven weight rigged with a number 4 barbless tan and cream bead chain Merkin on 8 pound in the rack ready to go. Sue was putting on a new leader. We had not discussed our game plan as yet, when a pair of bonefish tailed just out of casting distance. I slid over the side and began to stalk into good position for a cast. Even as I locked my focus on my target fish, I could see half a dozen more pods of fish in my peripheral vision. This was definitely going to be the best of the best of days!

I made an easy cast into the fish's area of awareness and he heard it land. One twitch of the crab and the bonefish pounded the fly. I cleared the line and turned to grin at Sue and Audley who watched from the skiff. By then I had refocused on the bonefish, which had about 40 yards of string on me. Next I heard the engine crank as Sue and Audley jumped to plane and headed down the channel. Subconsciously, I assumed they were going to the other end of the flat and work fish back towards me as the tide rose and it would maximize our fishing time and number of shots. Way cool!

Then the bonefish started right and taking a little more line. One single mangrove stalk was growing on this area of the flat and my bonefish was headed straight for it. There were dozens of other bonefish blowing out all around us. More were tailing everywhere. My bonefish wrapped the eight pound tippet once around the mangrove, popped the line and idled off to join a group of his buddies. No problem mon, plenty more where he came from and I got the best out of that fish anyway!

I reeled the line in and reached down to grab some tippet from my fanny pack and re rig but there was no fanny pack! There was nothing. In the excitement I had not put the pack on before leaving the boat. So here I am, starting out one of the best of the best trips ever under the "one third rule", fish tailing everywhere, perfect weather and tide, a great fly rod and no flies, no tippet no nothing! That is nothing but three quarters of a mile to wade back to the boat and my equipment! I yelled and waived my hands at Sue and Audley. They waved back from three quarters of a mile away.

After I slogged noisily, spooking bonefish right and left for about fifty yards my temperature dropped back to normal and my frustration receded. I was going to salvage this fiasco and being one to roll with the punches, I decided to suck it up and learn something. Without the distraction of trying to catch fish, I probably learned more about bonefish feeding and movements in the next hour than most people absorb in years! The one thing that surprised me was how loudly bonefish can laugh. It was a great trip!

CHAPTER XIV

Flyroding for Tarpon—My Proudest Catch

by Billy Pate

For a number of years the tarpon fishing in Homosassa on Florida's west coast was spectacular in both number and size. For several consecutive years the month of May there would allow me to jump over 200 tarpon each year. Over the years that I have fished there, I was able to put over 3,000 in the air, and 99.8% returned to the water to swim again since I have always tried to maintain and increase the population of sport fish.

The few tarpon that I kept there were believed to be world records on the flyrod. They included two world records on fly with 16 pound test leader tippet. One was 182 pounds and the other 188 pounds. Another was a flyrod record of 155 pounds on 12 pound tippet.

Then there was a tarpon I hooked while making an instructional video film with the 3M Company. The fish was hooked in the late morning. By late afternoon the tarpon had taken us twenty-five miles to the south and I had not been able to get it closer than thirty feet from the boat for 9 ½ hours on 16 pound tippet. The photographers were shooting with film not video tape, and when the sun hit the horizon in the west they began to put away their cameras saying there was not enough light for them to continue filming.

I pleaded with them to please take a chance and continue to film because my guide Lee Baker and I believed the fish was big enough to become a new world record, but they said there was no use. Lee had the 8 foot straight gaff in his hand (International Game Fish Association fly fishing rules did not allow a flying gaff with a detachable head) and we decided to make a desperation effort to capture it for weighing back at the dock. I took a chance on breaking my leader to get the fish close enough to gaff and Lee sank the gaff in the tarpon. One second later I was looking at the soles of Lee's feet and he went flying through the air holding onto the gaff and into the water. Oh, if we had just gotten close to him a few minutes earlier! The fish went down and Lee held on, then the fish tried to make a small jump while Lee was still under the water and holding on. What a picture that would have been! The tarpon swam toward our nearby camera and sound boat a few yards away. The sound man was a big, young, strong professor from Oregon. I screamed to him to take off his watch and take out his wallet and jump in and grab Lee, who was still holding on, around the waist. He did and it slowed the fish down almost to a stop. I cranked up my boat and guided it towards the fish with one hand and then with my legs so that I could reel in line. I cut the engine off as we got near the two men and the fish and its momentum carried me to Lee. The fish had stopped so Lee handed me the gaff which I held with one hand and I held the rod with the other. Lee climbed in the boat and together we hauled the giant tarpon into the boat.

It was just about dark now and we had 25 miles to run in the dark in waters where we had never driven at night before. There are giant rocks in many places only a foot or so under water. We were scared. Luckily with slow driving we finally found the mouth of the Homosassa River and we reached the scales at the dock about 11:30 at night.

We woke up the keeper of the scales and pulled the giant up. But what a disappointment! It weighed 185 pounds, three pounds lighter than my existing tarpon record on fly. The next morning I weighed myself and found that I had lost 10 pounds! The thought immediately dashed through my mind: How much did the tarpon lose in that battle?

So now we come to the story about another tarpon that is the one that became my proudest catch, even more than the one I have just related. My skiff has a front tower for the angler similar to the poling platform in the rear of the boat. There are two electric motors on the rear of my boat that are used when fighting fish with a guide. But, I also had on the front platform as well as the rear one, foot controls for controlling the on/off switch of each electric motor.

To turn the boat to the right, I cut off the right hand side electric motor, and to turn the boat to the left, I cut off the left hand electric motor. One morning when the fish were there in good numbers, I didn't have a guide booked so I decided to go out by myself and fish from the front platform and control my direction by using the foot pedals. Most of the tarpon that day were concentrated in an area about 5 miles north and south, and about a mile or two east and west. I had swung around to the south side of the concentration by running way outside of the mass of fish because I expected them to be moving south and I didn't want to scare the fish for anyone.

All of a sudden I saw a group of about 15 tarpon moving slowly toward me going south, and they were all very large. I cutoff the electric motors and cast to the lead fish that seemed to have a giant girth. The tarpon gulped down the fly, I set the hook, and when it jumped my heart beat fast because it did have a giant girth. It hit the water and it turned north with the rest of the group following. I got the electric motor going fast with a control switch strapped to my waist, and then started to follow and put pressure on the fish. It was heading north toward the group of around 25 to 30 boats. Several of the boats had seen the jump I learned later and everyone thought it was a very big tarpon.

The fish ran up through several boats and jumped three times. The radio in my pocket started getting calls. "You've got a mighty big one on", they said. I couldn't do much talking as I had to concentrate on fighting the fish and following its fast path with the electric motors. The tarpon then turned out to sea as they usually do and I followed for a couple of hours. The problem then was a west wind that I was having to head directly into, and it would blow me off course constantly. Finally the fish turned back to the east after its fellow tarpon swam away too fast for it to go with them because of the pressure of my line.

As I started getting closer on the fish in its easterly direction with the wind behind us, I saw that it was very wide. As we came back near the concentration of boats the fish jumped twice more near my boat. I started getting more radio calls saying, "I'll come help you and gaff the fish for you. It sure looks big enough for a record." I expressed my thanks and said I hadn't gotten the fish on its side yet. A boat started more or less following me, and its guide was a big, strong young man. When I finally got the fish on its side for a few moments, he called to say he was coming to help.

I looked in my back compartment and found my lip gaff and I thought to myself, "I'm going to see if I can lip gaff this big tarpon myself. With that girth it looks like a world record." Then it was easier said than done. Holding the rod in my left hand and the lip gaff

in my master right hand and spreading the two hands as far as possible, I couldn't quite reach the tarpon on the other side of the boat because of the big bend of the rod. So, I took a chance and lunged at the fish's open mouth. I was lucky and hooked him. Taking another chance, I dropped my rod and reel in the boat to put my left hand on the gaff also as the tarpon was starting to twist around. In the background I could see the other boat coming toward me and the angler friend had his camera in his hand taking pictures. I pulled the fish to the side of the boat and tried to pull it in. No luck. I was amazed at its girth so I put one foot up on the gunnel and strained with all my might. And it happened! I got it in! I immediately reached for a tape measure and started trying to measure the girth of the twisting fish. Finally I read it. 45 ¾ inches. My 188 pound record had a 43 inch girth, but this one seemed a little shorter. What should I do?

The other boat was real close to me now and the guide yelled, "How the heck did you get that fish in the boat all by yourself? What can I do to help now?" I don't know how I was able to do it alone, but I really wanted to try. I said, "You could help me by reading this tape measure and suggesting what I should do." Without a pause he said, "45 ¾ inches, take it in and weigh it. That's a very big tarpon." His angler friend was snapping pictures and I was on my radio calling the dockmaster to have some scales ready quickly.

I looked at the fish in disbelief. I couldn't believe what had happened, all by myself. But the fish looked a little short to have such a big girth. I crossed my fingers and cranked up the boat. "Thanks so much for your offer of help guys, and I'll see you back at the dock."

The dock was already crowded with people when I arrived. We hung the fish on the scales and checked the weight. Only 173 pounds. My heart sank. Just a bit too short for such a big girth! But then I related the story of its catch to the folks around and they were just amazed that I had done all of that completely by myself. I began to think: I am more proud of catching that tarpon than my two official world record tarpon of 182 and 188 pounds. I felt bad that I had kept a fish that wasn't a world record but I sincerely thought that it would be. And as I look back, I'm still the proudest of that tarpon of all the fish that I have ever caught.

CHAPTER XV

Last Cast

My interest and fascination with bonefishing started long ago and long before I had ever seen one first. I grew up in Battle Creek, Michigan, a long way from any bonefish flats. The fascination started when my father, who taught me the ins and outs of fresh water fishing in Michigan in the 50's, would also relay stories his friend John Shaw would tell him about the tarpon and bonefishing trips John would take to the Florida Keys.

John would go fishing in the spring and summer with his friends from Kalamazoo, Joel Shepherd Sr. and Henry Shakespeare, founder of the Shakespeare fishing equipment company. They would usually fish with guide Hank Brown and other guides of the day who had no problem creating the kind of experience from which legendary fish tales are made of.

I hadn't really thought too much about this until just a few days before completing this book. The occasion that served as a catalyst was the memorial service for my mother in Battle Creek. She died at age 93 and she was still sharp as a tack (there maybe hope for me). John was kind enough to come to the service to pay his respects. When we spoke, he also made a point of acknowledging the work I had been doing at and with BTU. This gave a good reason for me to explain that my bonefish addiction was really all his fault. I went on to inquire if he was still doing fishing in the Keys.

John got a pleasant far away look in his eyes and said, "Not much, I can't cast a big rod anymore you know". He said Hank Brown had called him last summer to say the fish were really thick and there was no one around, and suggested John come down for some fishing. John went, and they headed out for the renowned tarpon spot called "the pocket". When they reached their spot, the fish were "all stacked up" as John put it. Hank said to John, "You know I can't pole like I use to." John replied, "That's OK, I can't cast like I used to."

So the two old friends sat their contentedly watching the fish work as they recounted old days. They had a spectacular day with out ever wetting a line.

Is this a great sport or what? Thanks John for planting the seed.

POST SCRIPT

Exactly what the future holds for the sport we are passionate about no one can know for sure, but current trends in established fisheries like Florida and the Bahamas would appear to be in serious decline.

Fishing pressure may ultimately take care of itself as people will stop fishing if they aren't catching fish. Regrettably that seems an inappropriate solution for several reasons; it may be too late to reverse at that point, negative economic impact, and hopefully fishing pressure is either not the cause of the demise or at least not a large contributing factor.

It is my strong belief that Bonefish & Tarpon Unlimited (BTU), or organizations like BTU can be the salvation key to and improvement. They provide a vehicle to: aggregate private and public funding, provide research oversight and direction, a voice and advocate to government for appropriate regulatory support, and a vehicle for outreach and knowledge dissemination.

The challenge and focus of the current research supported by BTU is to provide general understanding of the life cycle and behavior and analysis of the habitat to ultimately isolate the factor or factors that are most limiting the number of adult fish in the fishery. If these factors can be identified, it is highly probably the effective action can be taken to reverse them and increase the adult population as has happened in trout and salmon fisheries.

All of those who have been involved with this book are Founding Members and strong supporters of BTU. If you are not, we encourage you to check the BTU website at www.tarbone.org to learn more about BTU. The organization's current need and challenge is to provide a sustained level of funding for research. A start-stop funding profile will simply not attract the quality of research or research personnel necessary to do this job. The answer is for our supporters to make a 4-year pledge of support so that BTU can in turn make a forward commitment to the research groups, and we encourage you to consider just that.

Looking forward to working with you on Bonefish & Tarpon Unlimited to insure that one you catch a big one, and your grandchildren do as well. Please join the cause at www.tarbone.org or mail to 24 Dockside Lane, # 83, Key Largo, FL 33037.

*Photo of a bonefish by Dr. Jerry Ault, University of Miami,
Rosenstiel School of Marine and Atmospheric Science.*

Bonefish & Tarpon Unlimited's Mission Statement

To support projects and research to help understand, nurture, and enhance a healthy Bonefish and Tarpon population.

BONEFISH & TARPON UNLIMITED

Founding Members

Teri Adams	Manny Fernandez	Billy Pate*
Fred Allen	Russ Fisher*	Jodi Pate
Terri Andrews	Susan Fitzgerald	Kaye Pearson
Jim Anson	Pat Ford	Chris Poncon
Stu Apte	Frank Fowler	Dick Pope, Jr.
Dr. Jerry Ault	Tom Gibson	Norwood Rahming
Suzan Baker	Curt Gowdy	Tim Reed
Lee Baker	Doug Hannon	Mindy Rich
Matt Bell	Jeff Storm Harkavy	Robert Rich
Marsha Bierman	Dr. Guy Harvey	Bill Rowley
Jim Bokor	Mina Hemingway	Rick Ruoff
Tim Borski	George Hommell, Jr.	Ansil Saunders
Curtis Bostick	Rick Howard	Dave Savage
Carlene Brennen	Mitch Howell	Bert Scherb
Hank Brown	Dr. Robert Humston	Norman Schwarzkopf
Henry Caimotto	Tom James	Joel Shepherd*
Jeff Cardenas	Paul Tudor Jones*	Adelaide Skoglund*
Mark Castlow	Ted Juracsik	Steve Sloan
Billy Causey	Glenda Kelley	Eddie Smith, Jr.*
Don Causey	Doug Kelly	Mike Smith *
C. D. Clarke	Amy Knowles	Mark Sosin
Vaughn Cochran	Lefty Kreh	Bob Sousa
Joe Costello	Rupert Leadon	John Squitero
Andy Coetzee	Mike Leech	E. Roe Stamps*
Jack Curlett	Alberto Madaria	Steve Stanley
Bill Curtis	Tim Mahaffey	Henry Stern
Larry Dahlberg	Roger Martin	Paul Swacina
John Davidson	Jeff McFadden	Donna Teeney
Tom Davidson, Sr.*	Steve McGrath	Jim Teeney
Tom Davidson, Jr.	Gary Merriman	Raiford Trask, III
Dr. John Dean	Andy Mill	Joan Vernon
Dave Denkert	Bruce Miller	Rufus Wakeman
Dr. Michael Domeier	George Mitchell	Millard Wells

James Donofrio   Sandy Moret   Raleigh Werking
John Donofrio   Sue Moret   Christine Todd Whitman
Pat Dorsy   Johnny Morris   (Honorary)
Thomas L. duPont   Joel Moxey   Karl Wickstrom
Gary Ellis   Rick Murphy   Dick Williams
Bob Epstein   Neal Myers*   Bill Willson*
Dick Farmer*   George R. Neugent Jeff "Gator" Wilson
Chico Fernandez   Darrick Parker   E. Carlton Wilton, Jr.*
                                      Joan Salvato Wulff

* Life Sponsor

BIBLIOGRAPHY

Shallow Water Angler. Spring 2004
       Boat Tech Article—Proper Props.

The Bonefish by George Reiger
       Meadow Run Press. Copyright 1990

Fly Fishing the Flats by Barry & Cathy Beck
       Stackpole Books

Saltwater Fly Fishing Magic by Neal & Linda Rogers
       Earth & Great Weather Publishers

Bonefishing with a Fly by Randall Kaufmann
       Western Fisherman's Press

Bonefishing by Randall Kaufmann
       Western Fisherman's Press

Shadows on the Flats by Chet Reneson & Ed Gray
       Willow Creek Press

Salt Water Fly Fishing by Joe Brooks
       Putnam

Fly Fishing for Bonefish by Dick Brown
       Lyons Press

Bonefish Fly Patterns by Dick Brown
       Lyons Press

Fly Fishing in Salt Water by Lefty Kreh
       Lyons Press

Flats Fishing by Jan Maizler
       Vantage Publishing

Florida Sportsman—February 1990 issue